stress relief

Marie Borrel

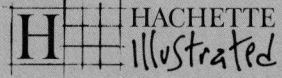

1 >>> 20 TIPS

contents

introduction 4
how to use this book 7
just how stressed are you? 8

useful addresses 124
index 125
acknowledgements 126

Note: The information and recommendations given in this book are not intended to be a substitute for medical advice. Consult your doctor before acting on any recommendations given in this book. The authors and publisher disclaim any liability, loss, injury or damage incurred as a consequence, directly or indirectly, of the use and application of the contents of this book.

01	respect your biological clock	12
02	rediscover the pleasure of eating	14
03	make sure you get enough magnesium	16
04	eat fruit and vegetables	18
05	give up stimulants	20
06	control your appetite	22
07	don't skip breakfast	24
08	get a good night's sleep	25
09	avoid taking medication	26
10	take a walk in the countryside	28
11	try hebal remedies	30
12	take a trip to the swimming pool	32
13	spend time with your friends	34
14	yawn, even in company	35
15	laughter is a great tonic	36
16	caress your feet	38
17	return to water, the source of life	40
18	take a walk on the sunny side	42
19	coat yourself in essential oils	44
20	give yourself a boost with wheatgerm	46
	case study	47

21 >>> 40 TIPS

41 >>> 60 TIPS

21	breathe deeply	50
22	learn the best position	52
23	imagine you're a tree	54
24	practise the art of the siesta	56
25	breathe a mouthful of pure air	58
26	try out some oriental dancing	60
27	run, jump, move…	61
28	stretch like a cat	62
29	learn relaxation techniques	64
30	listen to the music	66
31	learn to meditate	68
32	try zen	70
33	listen to the sound of silence	72
34	breathe through your skull	73
35	be a tiger in spring	74
36	speak the language of flowers	76
37	think homeopathy	78
38	take vitamins!	80
39	let massage improve your life	82
40	the finer points of acupuncture	84
	case study	85

41	think positive	88
42	be the star in your own movies	90
43	learn to love yourself	92
44	stop feeling guilty	94
45	set yourself reasonable targets	96
46	take your time	98
47	accept your failures	100
48	choose your friends carefully	102
49	don't be mean with compliments	103
50	learn to communicate better	104
51	don't let yourself be manipulated	106
52	express your emotions	108
53	dare to let go	110
54	spare some time for yourself	112
55	let the words flow from your pen	114
56	play several roles	115
57	discover the child within you	116
58	get into training	118
59	don't be ashamed of running away	120
60	words, words, words	122
	case study	123

intro
stress alert

At one time or another we have all been in a situation where we have felt helpless and completely unable to cope. We feel weak, and at a loss about what to do next. We are sometimes no longer even sure what is troubling us so much. We feel strangely tired, as if there is a heavy weight on our shoulders. We sleep badly, and our appetite fluctuates – first we lose it, and then we suddenly start eating like a ravenous animal so that we end up making ourselves feel sick. We are irritable and have a tendency to fly into a temper with other people over the smallest thing. Afterwards, we can hardly believe we have been so unfair, and feel guilty.

The name for this condition is stress. It is something that indiscriminately affects all social categories and all ages. Both the unemployed person anxious about the future and the senior manager, bowed down by the weight of his responsibilities, experience it. Likewise it affects both the mother worried about her children, and the top model trying to conceal the effects of the passing of time.

Friend or foe?

Stress is not merely destructive however. It has its good and bad sides, and human life would be impossible without it. The word does, in fact, mean two very different things. Firstly, it refers to all the pressures that incite us to respond and adapt to our environment: cold, hunger and danger motivated our remote, prehistoric ancestors to develop ways of adapting to their natural habitat, opening the way to progress and understanding. The word suggests our human endurance and ability to respond to pressure. This positive side of stress stimulates us to act, react and survive but, on the other hand, it can make us introspective, unhappy and ill. Many common symptoms result from this state of psychological and emotional tension, such as insomnia, migraine, digestive problems and a general feeling of being run down.

Everyone tolerates a different level of stress

This has led some specialists to conclude that there is 'good' stress and 'bad' stress. However, it is a little simplistic to see the problem in this way, because what matters is not so much the cause of stress but how we react to it. One person will easily handle continual unfair reprimands from a bad-tempered boss, whilst another will be depressed by them. The same is true of money worries, romantic disappointments and overwork. We all have our own particular level of resistance to stress, which usually results from our past experiences. Even when faced with intense pain that no one can escape, like the death of a loved one, we all react differently. This is just as well, because it enables us to adapt better to the situation.

The fight or flight response

We all have the same biological equipment for reacting to stress: a response strategy in three phases that our bodies have developed. When something threatening suddenly takes us by surprise, our body prepares for action – our heart beats more quickly, we breathe more rapidly and more blood than usual flows to the organs that most need it (the muscles for running away, the brain for making decisions). This is the alarm phase. The orders preparing us for action are issued by our hormones.

If the stress continues, the body, unable to maintain this level of activity for a very long time, enters the second or resistance phase. It now tries to return its secretions and functions to close to normal levels. We feel as if nothing in particular is happening but our body remains alert and is working intensely, though invisibly. This is the most insidious and dangerous phase.

Eventually, if this situation lasts too long, we suddenly enter the third phase, when the organism needs rest and starts failing to cope. We suddenly feel tired, exhausted, our vital functions are disturbed, we become gloomy and depressed.

A graduated programme of action

Fortunately our lives are not determined only by external circumstances and the way our body functions – we can make a difference ourselves in various ways. Firstly, we can keep our bodies fit in order to resist stress more effectively (through sport, healthy eating, herbs etc.). Next, we can learn how to deal with more acute problems by using natural techniques (such as yoga, relaxation and massage). Finally, when we seem hopelessly trapped in a stressful situation and the previously-used strategies are no longer working, we can seek the root of the problem. Why are we in such an uncomfortable situation? To what extent are we responsible? How can we change our own behaviour? If we cannot change our circumstances, we can always change the way we consider and respond to them.

In this way, and this way only, can we benefit from stress whilst experiencing none of its disadvantages. We can profit from the stimulation, imagination and creativity it produces without sinking into physical and mental exhaustion.

Everyone can put together an anti-stress programme that suits his or her lifestyle!

how to use this book

This book offers a made-to-measure programme, which will enable you to deal with your own particular problem. It is organized into four sections:

- **A questionnaire** to help you to assess the extent of your problem.
- **The first 20 tips** that will show you how to change your daily life in order to prevent problems and maintain health and fitness.
- **20 slightly more radical tips** that will develop the subject and enable you to cope when problems occur.
- **The final 20 tips** which are intended for more serious cases, when preventative measures and attempted solutions have not worked.

At the end of each section someone with the same problem as you shares his or her experiences.

You can go methodically through the book from tip I to 60 putting each piece of advice into practice. Alternatively, you can pick out the recommendations which appear to be best suited to your particular case, or those which fit most easily into your daily routine. Or, finally, you can choose to follow the instructions according to whether you wish to prevent stress problems occuring or cure ones that already exist.

●●● FOR YOUR GUIDANCE

> A symbol at the bottom of each page will help you to identify the natural solutions available.

- **Herbal medicine, aromatherapy, homeopathy, Dr Bach's flower remedies** – how natural medicine can help.
- **Simple exercises** – preventing problems by strengthening your body.
- **Massage and manipulation** – how they can help to promote well-being.
- **Healthy eating** – all you need to know about the contribution it makes.
- **Practical tips for your daily life** – so you can prevent instead of having to cure.
- **Psychology, relaxation, Zen** – advice to help you be at peace with yourself and regain serenity.

> A complete programme that will solve all your health problems.
Try it!

just how stressed are you?

Read the following statements and tick box **A** if you are seldom affected by these problems, box **B** if you are regularly affected and box **C** if you suffer from them permanently.

A	B	C	
A	B	C	I feel irritable first thing in the morning for no apparent reason.
A	B	C	I have a problem sleeping.
A	B	C	I sometimes lose my temper over little or nothing.
A	B	C	I find people close to me (work colleagues, children, parents etc) irritating.
A	B	C	I don't bother about what I eat.
A	B	C	I find it hard to express how I feel.
A	B	C	I find it hard to relax.
A	B	C	I am dissatisfied with my way of life.
A	B	C	I am terrified of change and scared stiff anything new.
A	B	C	I am always short of time.

If you answered mainly **A**s, then tips **1** to **20** are the most suitable ones for you.

If you have answered mainly **B**s, go directly to tips **21** to **40**.

If you have answered mainly **C**s, turn immediately to tips **41** to **60** – there's no time to lose!

》》 **No one is totally free from stress.** We all experience periods of tension and tiredness that are hard to handle.

》》》》 **All you need to do is regularly take steps to deal with them.** Firstly, food – eating the right amount and healthily is a good way of combating stress. Next, exercise – move that body, get plenty of fresh air, go swimming. Finally, pamper yourself with regular and relaxing beauty care.

》》》》》》 **Make these 20 tips a regular part of your daily life,** and you will sail through the little stresses of the day without even noticing them!

01 respect your biological clock

Time is not merely something displayed on the face of a clock. A series of precise rhythms also occur inside our bodies. Being aware of them and respecting them is the first step towards a calmer, more relaxed life.

Visible and invisible rhythms

Our body is governed by unchanging biological rhythms. Some are easily noticed: in the evening, there always comes a time when we feel sleepy; the next morning, there always comes a time when we wake up. Many other functions follow similar chronological patterns – digestion, the secretion of hormones, alertness, the reproduction of cells, the production of cholesterol etc.

●●● DID YOU KNOW?

> Chronobiology is the name given to the branch of medicine which studies our biological rhythms. Chronopharmacology examines the influence of these cycles on the taking of drugs and medicines.

> It appears, for example, that aspirin works quicker and causes less stomach acid at 10 pm. Anaesthetics are thought to have more effect at around 3 pm.

Keep a personal diary

To remain cool, calm and collected in all circumstances, to avoid running out of nervous and intellectual energy, to avoid exhaustion and unnecessary stress you need to learn to obey these rhythms. The only way to do this is to keep a check on them. For a few days write down in a notebook the times when you feel hungry, mentally drained, physically tired, when you suddenly feel like going to sleep and so on. At the end of a week you will see clear patterns emerging. Try, as soon as you can, to organize your life around these patterns. You will feel fitter and will already have removed one recurrent source of stress from your daily life.

> Similarly, the body is more or less sensitive to toxic substances according to the time of day. Experiments have shown that a poison injected into rats killed 80% of them at 4.30 pm, but only 10% at half past midnight!

KEY FACTS

∗ Our mental and physical functions conform to a number of natural rhythms.

∗ By respecting these natural rhythms, we can avoid a source of daily stress.

∗ To learn about the pattern of these rhythms, keep a diary of when you feel hungry, tired, energetic, sleepy etc.

02 rediscover the pleasure of eating

The very same meal can be a source of pleasure or stress according to its setting and atmosphere. What is on your plate is not all that matters. So get into the habit of eating in a calm and cheerful atmosphere!

Noisy restaurant or sunny terrace?

Healthy eating means not only taking care over what you eat but also over how you eat: who you eat with, the atmosphere in which the meal takes place and so on. The same dish tastes different depending on whether you gulp it down in a noisy, smoky restaurant with your mind still full of worries or share it with friends on a sunny terrace with

●●● DID YOU KNOW?

> Rediscovering the pleasure of eating involves relearning how to taste. Eating frozen or factory-produced food at top speed does not allow our taste buds to get to work and they gradually lose their sensitivity.

> To re-educate them, do your best to eat fresh, natural foods, taking time to really savour their tastes: fresh fruit, crunchy vegetables, grilled fish, pure oils etc.

birds singing in the background. It does not have the same effect on your metabolism either. Above all, it does not have the same influence on your mood. In the first case, the meal sustains your mood of tension and nervousness, in the second, it relieves it.

Lunch wisely and have dinner with friends

Lunch: even if you haven't much time, make lunch a moment for yourself. Try not to waste the opportunity for a calm moment during the day: don't accept invitations that you don't want, find a place where you can relax, choose healthy, tasty food rather than fatty, sugary dishes. When you rush a meal, all tense and anxious, your digestion and metabolism will be disturbed.

Dinner: alternate, according to what you want, quiet meals alone or with the family, and convivial dinners with friends. Don't have the television on during the meal (especially if you have children!). Put on some soft music instead.

> These natural tastes will gradually revive your palate. You will then begin to appreciate their blends again and enjoy your food even more!

KEY FACTS

∗ The very same meal can be a source of stress or relaxation according to the circumstances in which it is eaten.

∗ Avoid noisy, smoky places and share the time with people you like.

∗ Ban television at mealtimes.

03 make sure you get enough magnesium

Magnesium is the main fuel of the brain and central nervous system. When we are stressed we use up enormous amounts of it. When we do not get sufficient, we become irritable and nervous. Make sure your diet contains enough magnesium.

Less anxiety, more sleep

Magnesium is one of the most essential minerals. Our body needs it to successfully complete many tasks: to convert lipids and carbohydrates into energy, to produce antibodies that protect us from diseases, to regulate body temperature and, above all, to resist stress! We have a vital need for magnesium to transmit nerve impulses through the nerves and

●●● DID YOU KNOW?

> Calcium works hand-in-hand with magnesium. Calcium is not only a mineral found in bones! It also acts as regulator of the central nervous system.

> The daily requirement of magnesium is 300–400 mg.

spinal cord as well as the brain. Without enough magnesium we become agitated, irritable and nervous. We do not sleep well. We can no longer tolerate the slightest annoyance. It acts as a sort of natural sedative, controlling anxiety and helping us to sleep.

Wholemeal bread, dark chocolate and mineral water

The recommended daily intake of magnesium for an adult is 300–400 mg. However, many factors can increase the amount we need: strong emotions, distress, fear, certain drugs like antibiotics, and even cold weather.

Good sources of magnesium include wholemeal bread, wholemeal cereals, dark chocolate, nuts (almonds, hazelnuts) and pulses (haricot beans, chickpeas). It is also found in some mineral waters. If you are going through a stressful time, make these foods a part of your daily diet. Although they contain plenty of calories, they will not make you fat if you take care to adjust your other food intake.

KEY FACTS

* Magnesium is vital for the efficient transmission of nerve impulses.

* It is found in nuts, pulses, wholemeal bread and dark chocolate.

* Don't forget that some mineral waters are very rich in magnesium.

04 eat fruit and vegetables

To deal with stressful situations our body needs an adequate reserve of nutriments like carbohydrates, vitamins and minerals. Where could we get them more naturally and easily than from the food we eat daily? First of all, think fruit and vegetables.

DID YOU KNOW?

> The contents of fruit and vegetables all differ. However, you don't need a calculator to ensure that you are eating all your body needs every day.

> Just vary regularly the colour of the produce you eat, because the different colours are largely due to different vitamins and minerals.

Make vegetables part of every meal

Fresh fruit and vegetables are rich mines of vitamins and minerals. They provide almost all we need. Foods of animal origin are better sources of iron and vitamins B12, D and A, but otherwise fruit and vegetables provide much of what we need, plus other nutriments as well: fibre to improve digestion (constipation makes us irritable); carbohydrates to provide energy for the tissues (without them we soon get tired); water to help prevent dehydration (90% of some vegetables consists of water).

We ought to eat some fruit and/or vegetables at every meal. If you have got out of this good habit, now is the time to do something about it. Spare the time to go to the market to choose fresh fruit and vegetables. Organic produce is just as good nutritionally as produce grown using chemical fertilizers and pesticides but without the risk of toxic residues in the food.

Eat raw or gently steamed

Vitamins are fragile and temperamental: some oxidize on contact with air, some dissolve in water and are lost, whilst others are damaged by heat. To be sure of not losing even the smallest amount, eat at least two portions of uncooked salad vegetables and two fresh fruits daily. Wash them under the tap but never soak them in water. When cooking vegetables, choose the more gentle methods (steaming or a low flame). If you do boil vegetables, keep the water to use for a soup or as the base of a sauce: it is full of vitamins!

KEY FACTS

* Fruit and vegetables provide us with vitamins, minerals, carbohydrates, fibre and water.

* It's better to choose organic.

* Eat five portions of fruit or vegetables daily.

* Vary the colours in order to eat a range of vitamins and minerals.

> For example orange-coloured fruit and vegetables (melons, carrots, apricots) contain beta-carotene, which is converted to vitamin A in the gut, whilst green-leaved vegetables (spinach, cress, cabbages) contain calcium.

05 give up stimulants

To keep going in times of stress we tend to make a beeline for stimulants: coffee, tobacco and alcohol. Some keep us awake, others help us to switch off in the evening. These are very bad habits and their side-effects are more harmful than they might seem.

Insomnia, nightmares, trembling

We tend to drink coffee, which came originally from Yemen, morning, noon and night. Coffee addicts drink up to ten cups a day, if not more. Initially, coffee certainly increases heart rate, stimulates the brain and improves learning and memory. This is all due to the caffeine. But this state of stimulation soon dies away. To regain it, we drink another cup.

● ● ● DID YOU KNOW?

> Alcohol depresses the central nervous system. Its well known effect in increasing conviviality is due to the release of inhibition rather than brain stimulation.

> The more alcohol you drink, the more quickly this effect arrives. By altering the chemistry of the brain, alcohol causes a sense of euphoria followed by an apparent mood of relaxation.

It's a vicious circle and there really are some people addicted to coffee. Drink more than 600mg, say four cups of strong coffee, and the caffeine causes insomnia, nightmares and trembling. When you are tired, it is much better to take a few minutes of genuine rest!

Don't pile one stress upon another!

Smoking is a way of trying to cure stress by giving yourself more stress. Lighting up a cigarette when we feel a strong emotion or annoyance certainly has a calming effect to begin with. However, this only lasts a short while and then we need another cigarette. Besides, as anyone who has tried to give up will tell you, there is hardly any situation more stressful! And then there are also the harmful effects of tobacco on our health.

If you smoke, decide to stop when things are calm so as not to pile stress upon stress. Get some help: support groups, homeopathy, the patch, acupuncture, auricular acupuncture etc.

> Don't be mistaken: excessive alcohol disturbs sleep and reduces its benefits. You may be tempted to drink alcohol when stressed. Don't. It will tend to make you more depressed in the long run.

KEY FACTS

* Coffee is a stimulant but it soon causes tiredness and makes you feel low.

* Tobacco is generally a danger to our health. Choose a time when life is calm to give up.

* Alcohol disturbs sleep and reduces its benefits.

06 control your appetite

Stress sometimes causes eating disorders that can take a hold and turn into real illnesses. To avoid anorexia or bulimia, come to terms with your appetite.

A ravenous appetite or none at all

We ought never eat too much or too little! Our body has regulatory and information mechanisms that enable us to know at any given moment what it needs in order to function. That is fine in theory but in practice it is not that simple. We sometimes have uncontrollable cravings for food or sudden losses of appetite because of the way we feel.

● ● ● DID YOU KNOW?

> It's our brain that gets hungry, not our stomach! As soon as our tissues are about to run short of some vital substance, the brain launches its emergency plan: empty stomach, over-salivation, tiredness, slight dizziness.

> Even when we are sleeping, our body uses up nutriments that have been stored away at mealtimes. This is especially true of the brain, which is a great consumer of sugar. As soon as it starts running short, it stimulates us to eat.

Stress can cause some people to eat well beyond the point where they are absolutely full, whilst others feel that their stomach has been closed up and have no appetite at all although their body is crying out for food. At times like these the body's messages are being jammed by emotions, tensions, distress and so on.

Taste and savour

Both too much and too little food disrupts our organism and prevents it from developing its usual strategies for adapting to stress. To be less disturbed by stress, we need to learn how to eat reasonably again.

Always listen carefully to your appetite. If you give yourself an extra treat even when you are no longer hungry, don't feel guilty but take the time to taste and enjoy it down to the very last mouthful. Then you won't want any more. If, on the other hand, you are not hungry, don't force yourself to eat. Try, however, to eat a little of something highly nutritious (royal jelly, honey, brewer's yeast, wheatgerm), which will provide your body with the bare minimum, while it waits for things to get better!

KEY FACTS

* Under stress some people binge on food, whilst others lose their appetite.

* Both too much and too little food disturbs the organism in times of stress.

* Try to accept what your appetite is telling you.

07 don't skip breakfast

It's the first meal of the day and perhaps the most important, especially during periods of stress. So take the time to have a good breakfast!

Replenish your reserves: at night our organism functions on the reserves built up during the day. Processes like breathing, heartbeat and the filtration of waste materials through the kidneys gradually exhaust them. In the morning the reserves need to be replaced. This is what breakfast does. Firstly, it restores energy to the body's organs, especially the brain, then it provides the muscles with proteins and finally, it supplies us with water and essential nutriments like vitamins, minerals and fatty acids.

A quarter of your daily calorie intake: that is what a good breakfast should be (400-500 calories). It must be balanced: an egg or some ham (proteins), cereals or bread (complex carbohydrates which are absorbed slowly), jam or honey (simple carbohydrates which are absorbed rapidly), butter (fatty acids), fruit juice or fresh fruit (vitamins), milk or natural yoghurt (calcium), a drink (tea or coffee). Above all, avoid too much sugar and fat (sweet pastries, sugary milk products).

● ● ● DID YOU KNOW?

> Breakfast is also a time when the family can be together. Afterwards, parents and children often leave each other for the rest of the day.
> All the more reason to take trouble over breakfast and eat the meal together at the table without hurrying.

KEY FACTS

* Breakfast restores the reserves of energy which are used up during the night.

* It should be a quarter of the daily calorie intake.

08 get a good night's sleep

Tired? Stressed? It's time to rest. The best rest occurs at night. It does not matter whether you go to bed early or late as long as you are obeying your own natural sleep pattern.

Happy nights: lack of sleep is, in itself, a source of stress. Worse still, when we do not get enough sleep or sleep badly, we are less able to resist daytime pressures and they upset us more than they would normally. To avoid this slow wearing down process, we need a good night's sleep. The answer is simple: learn to obey your natural sleep pattern.

Keep a sleep diary: the need for sleep obeys a precise biological clock which varies according to the individual. There is no firm rule: some people need nine or ten hours sleep, while others can get by on five or six. To understand your own biological clock, keep a sleep diary: every day make a note of when you begin to feel sleepy. After a few days you will see a pattern emerging. That is your bedtime!

● ● ● DID YOU KNOW?

> Sleep occurs in approximately one and a half hour cycles, which are repeated throughout the night. If you miss your bedtime, go to bed when you are ready and get up at the same time the next day.

> A short relaxation session before going to bed may help you to get to sleep more easily.

KEY FACTS

∗ Lack of sleep is a source of stress.

∗ To sleep well you need to keep to your personal sleep rhythms.

∗ Keep a diary to find out your ideal bedtime.

09 avoid taking medication

Psychotropic drugs like sleeping pills, tranquillizers and antidepressants are becoming increasingly popular all over the world. However, these drugs can have more drawbacks than advantages. They should be used only for very serious or prolonged cases of stress.

The vicious circle of dependence on prescribed drugs

All over the world the prescription of mood changing drugs is on the increase. However, these drugs, prescribed so liberally by some doctors, are far from being a panacea. They are accompanied by a large number of side-effects, some of which can be very harmful in the long term: drowsiness, memory loss, fatigue, loss of libido, nausea.

●●● DID YOU KNOW?

> If you have been taking mood-changing drugs for more than one year, you can ask your doctor to organize a programme of gradual withdrawal for you.

> Some natural forms of medicine, like homeopathy and herbal medicine, can be used to support withdrawal and make it less difficult.

But worse of all is the dependence they cause. Their benefits (control of anxiety, better sleep, lifting of depression) soon become less marked. To continue to feel the benefits, the doses may have to be increased, causing a vicious circle to develop. Some mood-changing drugs can be genuinely addictive. However, where disturbed sleep is associated with depression, anti-depressants can be very useful and treating the depression will restore the sleep rhythm to normal.

For a limited period only

These drugs have their uses during crises when we feel overwhelmed by circumstances. However, they cannot resolve our problems. The emotional and psychological pain is still there, even if temporarily anaesthetized. It does not deal with the underlying problem but buys time to deal with it.

Mood-changing drugs, which are issued on a doctor's prescription, must be taken for a limited period only. Sleeping tablets should be used one to three times a week; four weeks for tranquillizers. Anti-depressants may need to be taken for four to six months to consolidate their effect.

KEY FACTS

* Doctors are prescribing increasing quantities of mood-changing drugs.

* Sleeping pills, tranquillizers and antidepressants quickly become addictive.

* They should be reserved for urgent cases and used for a limited time only.

10 take a walk in the countryside

Physical exercise and fresh air are the best stress beaters. When it comes to unwinding, there is nothing to equal a walk in the woods or beside the sea. It is the ideal way of driving away unhappy thoughts, annoyances and physical tension.

Physically…

Physical exercise is the best and most natural anti-stress medicine. Add to that the open air and you've got the lot! However, to be beneficial and trouble-free, sport must be regular, moderate and suited to our physical capabilities. This is what makes walking the ideal sporting activity for people who are not naturally sporty.

●●● DID YOU KNOW?

> To ensure that walking effectively combats stress, there are some rules you must follow.

> Regularity: 20 minutes walking a day is better than one hour every now and then.

> Try to go for a walk at least four times a week.

If you walk at quite a brisk pace, you exercise all the muscles in your body and breathe more deeply. As a result, physical tension vanishes, breathing improves, the tissues receive more oxygen, blood circulation gets better, metabolic waste is disposed of more rapidly and the muscles and joints become more supple.

Mentally…

Meanwhile the rhythm of your footsteps will enable you to think more clearly. You can help by concentrating on details of the landscape around you, thus turning a walk in the countryside into a period of active meditation.
Finally, the contact with nature helps us to get problems into perspective: problems that sometimes seem insoluble until we stand back from them.

> Intensity: don't push yourself too hard and tire yourself too much.
> If you walk regularly your fitness, speed and strength will all improve.

KEY FACTS

* Physical activity in the open air is the best method of combatting stress.

* The body is freed from built-up tensions.

* Contact with nature encourages a meditative state of mind and puts our problems into perspective.

11 try herbal remedies

All over the world throughout the ages, people have used herbs to cure illnesses. Some varieties are particularly recommended as a natural way of dealing with the effects of stress. You can use them regularly and, unlike synthetic drugs, they will never cause dependency.

••• DID YOU KNOW?

> Herbal teas are usually drunk in the evening before going to bed. You should not drink more than three cups per day.

> If infusing a herb at night holds no charms for you, take plants in capsule or ampoule form.

Active natural principles

Do you have problems at work that are spoiling the rest of your life? Are you arguing with your partner? Are your children worrying you? Before you crack up, take a trip down to your local chemist or health food shop. There you will find herbs that will help you stay calm and sleep again at nights.

Medicinal herbs contain natural active principles, some of which have hypnotic, sedative or antidepressive effects and they can cure a lot of problems.

Anxious, unable to sleep, tired?

Here are some anti-stress stars:
- **marjoram:** calms and relieves nervousness, anxiety and aggressiveness.
(Put 1 tablespoon of the herb in 1 litre/ 1 3/4 pints of boiling water and infuse for 10 minutes);
- **valerian:** helps you to sleep and calms agitation and palpitations caused by stress.
(Put 1 tablespoon of chopped roots into 1/2 litre/8 fl oz of cold water, boil for 3 minutes and infuse for 10 minutes);
- **lemon balm:** calms nervousness and tones up the body to help it resist stress.
(Put 1 tablespoon of the herb in 1/2 litre/ 8 fl oz of boiling water and infuse for 10 minutes);
- **passionflower:** calms you when you feel tired and overwrought, and gives you a good night's sleep.
(Put 1 tablespoon of the herb in 1 cup of boiling water and infuse for 10 minutes).

> Capsules usually contain dry extracts or ground herbs, whilst ampoules contain liquid extracts.

KEY FACTS

* Some medicinal herbs have a sleep-inducing or sedative effect.

* Try lemon balm, passionflower, valerian or marjoram.

* If you don't like herbal teas, try more up to date forms like capsules or ampoules.

12 take a trip to the swimming pool

We spent the first nine months of our existence in lukewarm water. Plunging into it again triggers a calming, relaxing 'back to the womb' factor. Swimming also involves movement and a sense of weightlessness, so it's bound to combat stress!

Natural relaxation

We developed in a lukewarm liquid in the womb. For most of us this was a peaceful time: we were sheltered from noise and light and lulled by our mother's movements. When we jump into the tepid water of a swimming pool, it is natural for us to feel these sensations again. This is why the very act of bathing is relaxing.

DID YOU KNOW?

> Swimming is a genuine sporting activity and you should take no risks. For instance, avoid doing the backstroke if you suffer from back problems.

> If you haven't swum for a long time, go gently: none of your first three sessions should be more than thirty minutes long. Then add five minutes each session until you're swimming for forty-five minutes.

But there is more to it than that. When we are submerged, we float and escape the law of gravity. The brain does not need to work as hard, so we experience a natural sense of mental relaxation. Our muscles, bones and joints can take it easy too, which makes us feel physically relaxed.

Relaxed muscles, deep breathing

It is not just a matter of floating. You can move too! When we swim, the muscles of our entire body are allowed to work more gently. The muscles of the spinal column, often badly affected by stress, become less tight and tense. Lastly, when swimming, our breathing has to be in time with our movements, which makes us breathe more deeply and regularly. All this occurs and we don't even have to think about it!

> Don't force yourself to swim if you're not feeling well. All relaxation needs the element of pleasure to be effective.

KEY FACTS

* Because of the time we spent in the womb, water naturally induces physical and mental relaxation.

* Swimming works all our muscles.

* It is a genuine sporting activity and some precautions need to be taken.

13 spend time with your friends

During stressful periods we tend to become introverted and isolated, when we should be speaking to and seeing the people we like.

Human beings are social creatures. We must not forget this at times of crisis and stress, because there is nothing to be gained from staying at home constantly mulling over our problems. Of course, there are times when we hardly feel fit for company and believe we have nothing to say to anyone. However, that is putting too little trust in our ability to enjoy ourselves on the one hand and the patience of our friends on the other!

Taking our minds off our problems: it is not a question of having to see other people when we do not want to, but of breaking out of our isolation. This can help us to see things in a different light. We need to get rid of that devious sense of guilt that sometimes leads us to reject what we could enjoy, either because we feel we have no right to enjoy ourselves or because we fear being boring.
Finally, sharing our worries with a close friend enables us to stand back and see them in a different light. Don't forget that very often the solution is not far away, although we cannot see it.

••• DID YOU KNOW?

> Support groups are based upon the principles of sharing and friendship: they bring together people with the same problem.
> Experiences are shared, creating a network of support and helping to put an end to the sense of isolation.

KEY FACTS

* In times of stress, we are sometimes inclined to isolate ourselves.

* It's important not to be isolated.

* Sharing worries allows us to stand back from them.

14 yawn, even in company

Yawning is not the done thing! You put your hand in front of your mouth or, better still, stop yourself. Yet, when used in yoga, it is an excellent way of combatting stress.

A completely natural way to relax: yawning is breathing whilst involuntarily opening your mouth wide. It is a reflex action that occurs when we are sleepy, hungry or very bored. In India, it is a practice used by the yogis to achieve certain postures more effectively. Yawning is a healthy action caused by the body and not the mind. When we yawn, we are lowering all our defences and a wave of natural relaxation passes through us.

Don't suppress this physical impulse! Of course not but how do you yawn when you are neither hungry nor sleepy? Follow this advice:
- don't think about it, just let your animal side out;
- open your mouth wide;
- allow your yawn to come up, don't try to suppress it.

DID YOU KNOW?

> Sighing is caused by a similar mechanism. It is also a discharge of air that brings a feeling of relaxation and satisfaction.
> In both cases it is all a matter of breath: you are breathing in or out with special force.

KEY FACTS

* Yawning is a healthy breathing reflex action that calms and relaxes you.

* You should learn to yawn at will and should never suppress a yawn.

* Sighing is also a way of combatting stress.

15 laughter is a great tonic

After a good fit of the giggles, we feel relaxed, calm and free from tension. Some people even consider laughter as a genuine treatment for headaches and other kinds of pain. Quite apart from the amusement factor, laughter is the cause of many physical benefits.

Laughter does us a whole lot of good

Laughter involves a series of small, jerky exhalations caused by involuntary contractions of the diaphragm. This physiological explanation will not raise a laugh but laughter is also, as Rabelais wrote, 'the defining characteristic of man'. We laugh in response to many kinds of stimuli: intellectual (jokes, funny images, witty remarks) and physical

DID YOU KNOW?

> Laughter also has a social function. It involves sharing and communicating and so brings people together.

> The Dogon people of West Africa hold community laughter sessions. The North American Indians have healing clowns.

(tickling, laughing gas and so on). Whatever the cause, a burst of laughter does us a whole lot of good! Firstly, it relaxes us and secondly, it helps to drive away stress.

Tensions fade away

You have just heard a good joke? This is how your body reacts: you breathe more deeply; your gastric juices increase; your stomach contracts and your intestines work more rapidly; your liver and pancreas are 'massaged' by the diaphragm's contractions; the chemicals inside your brain are altered. The result of all this is that you breathe and digest better, your physical tensions fade away, you feel euphoric and you forget your worries. After a hilarious evening, you sleep better and wake up feeling good the next morning.

> The Dalai Lama, the temporal and spiritual leader of Tibet, says that laughing is his favourite hobby. He sees it as a state of mind and being and considers it as a blessing.

KEY FACTS

* A good burst of laughter relaxes you mentally and physically.

* Laughing alters the chemicals in your brain and causes a feeling of euphoria.

* After a hilarious evening, you sleep better and wake up feeling good in the morning.

16 caress your feet

We have a whole host of things on the soles of our feet: for instance, nerve and energy endings, and a 'return pump' to help circulation within the body. Massaging the sole activates several vital functions and, above all, removes accumulated stress. It can be done alone, with the family or with friends.

Marvels of living technology

Our feet do more than merely enable us to stand upright on the ground. These little marvels of bone-and-joint technology contain an incredible range of features that create a sense of well-being. Firstly, the sole of the foot is equipped with thousands of sensors, which provide information about such things as the ground, the temperature and the

●●● DID YOU KNOW?

> A thorough foot massage lasts about thirty minutes. Begin by massaging the whole of one foot, concentrating on each of the toes. Then take the foot between your hands, with your thumbs on the sole, and press down strongly on the chosen points, making little rotating movements. End with a gentle massage of the whole of the foot before moving on to the other one.

> To achieve even more relaxation you can use a massage oil containing essential oils. (See Tip 19).

humidity. It also has a kind of pump made up of a tight knot of muscles, blood vessels and lymphatic vessels. This pump helps the blood and lymph fluid to rise, against gravity, and return to the top of the body. We should pamper them if only to help them perform this task!

A moment of pure happiness

But that is not the main thing. According to the Chinese tradition of medicine, we have 'reflex zones' on the soles of our feet, each of which corresponds to a part of the body. They are in a sense projections, which, when massaged, can revive or soothe organs that are not functioning well.

As far as stress is concerned, a good massage of the whole foot helps to relax the muscles and the entire body. If you concentrate on the parts of the foot corresponding to the head, brain, endocrine glands, spinal cord and solar plexus, you will help your body to resist tension and your mind to get problems into perspective. And don't forget the pleasure it brings: a foot massage is a moment of pure happiness!

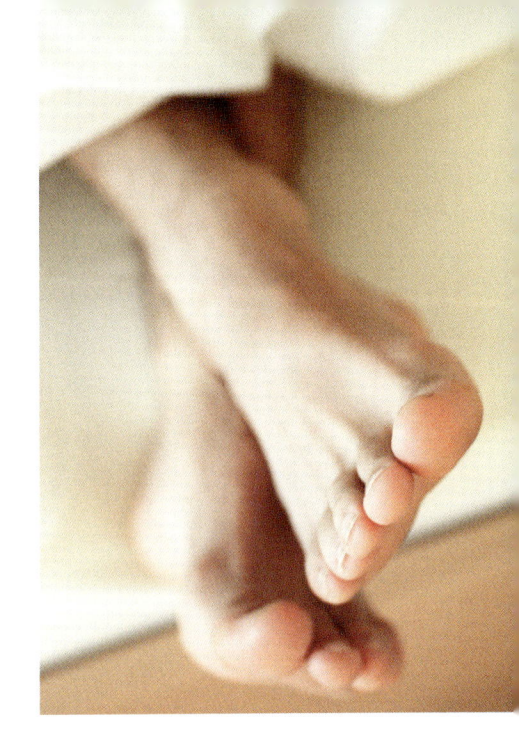

KEY FACTS

* On our feet there are reflex zones.

* To relieve stress we need to massage the zones corresponding to the brain, head, endocrine glands, spinal cord and solar plexus.

* A thorough foot massage lasts thirty minutes.

17 return to water, the source of life

We never drink enough of it! Water is vital if our body is to perform all its many functions and this is even truer in times of stress. To eliminate all the waste products of stress and provide us with the minerals we need, don't forget the need for water.

DID YOU KNOW?

> On average we should drink 1–1.5 litres ($1^3/_4$ –$2^1/_2$ pints) of water per day. Everyone has a different metabolism and might need more or less than that.

> Remember to drink before you feel really thirsty: when that alarm signal goes off, the body is already in a state of dehydration.

A litre and a half (2½ pints) per day

Water is as indispensable as the air we breathe. Seventy per cent of our body consists of this precious liquid. Even our bones, which look so solid, contain more than thirty per cent of it. We can go without eating for several weeks without doing ourselves irreparable harm but we cannot last for more than a few days without drinking.

Our food provides us with 1 litre (1¾ pints) of water per day but we lose 2.5 litres (4¼ pints) through urination, breathing and sweating. So we must consume the missing 1.5 litres (2½ pints) or risk getting dehydrated.

More stress, more waste

When we are under pressure, we must pay particular attention to the amount of water we drink for two reasons. Firstly, water is invo… nourishment to the tis… the excretory organs. … under stress, we sometim… unwell or preoccupied to eat properly. However, if you are …ell hydrated, you will feel better. Drink plain water rather than caffeinated beverages – they can make you feel more jittery. Fruit juices are high in sugars, so avoid these in excess.

> Make sure you find out how much water you need every day.

KEY FACTS

* Water is indispensable to life

* On average we need to drink 1.5 litres of water (2½ pints) per day.

* We need more water during moments of stress.

* Water provides us with vital minerals.

18 take a walk on the sunny side

The sun is not necessarily dangerous. Although it can harm the skin, it is good for our state of mind and general health. In moderation it helps the skin produce vitamin D, which is essential for strong healthy bones.

Sunlight, melatonin's best friend

That most people are in a better mood when it is fine weather than when the weather is very dull is far from a new discovery. There is a reason for this: natural light reaches our eyes and travels along the optic nerve to the brain where it is involved in the secretion of hormones that govern mood, in particular melatonin. This hormone is produced in

●●● DID YOU KNOW?

> Some cases of depression, of breakdown even, are due to lack of sunlight. This is called Seasonal Affective Disorder. It starts in October and stops spontaneously in the spring ... until the next autumn.

> The cure is simple: sunray treatment. Patients are placed under specially designed lamps which, unlike normal light bulbs, produce rays very similar to sunlight.

the pineal gland and is also responsive to light and dark. Its secretion fluctuates over 24 hours and it controls our internal biological rhythms, rather like the conductor of an orchestra. .

Walking in the open air compared with intensive sunbathing

To benefit from the sun does not mean exposing yourself to it for hours on end during the hottest part of the day. It should be enjoyed in moderation. A walk in the open air on a beautiful sunny day with your eyes wide open is better than an hour of intensive sunbathing with your eyes closed. Your skin will suffer less and you will feel in a much better mood. However, if you really like basking in the sun, choose the morning (before noon) or the late afternoon (after four o'clock). And don't forget to use a sun cream strong enough to protect your skin type.

> Some inhabitants of Scandinavian countries find winter a real psychological ordeal. Each year they sink into lethargy and melancholy, which disappear when the fine weather returns.

KEY FACTS

* Sunlight helps produce melatonin, which governs our moods.

* If you do expose yourself to the sun, don't forget to use sun cream to protect your skin.

* Artificial full spectrum lights are used as a treatment for winter depression.

19 coat yourself in essential oils

Essential oils are the concentrated form of plants with very potent qualities. When it comes to relaxing us, getting rid of our tensions, calming our overstretched nerves and pampering us to sleep, some of them can work wonders. Use them for massage, before sleep.

Two hundred times stronger than the plant itself

Essential oils are produced from aromatic plants. In other words, in addition to their actual therapeutic qualities, these plant extracts smell good as well! Whether you are using culinary herbs (basil, rosemary, cinnamon etc) or flowers (neroli, rose, ylang-ylang etc), their effectiveness is enhanced by their perfumes. Essential oils are obtained by

••• DID YOU KNOW?

> For relaxation: rosewood, lavender, jasmine.
> To improve sleep: ylang-ylang, neroli, marjoram.
> To combat tiredness: rosemary, lemon, basil.
> To calm anger: sandalwood, rosewood, neroli.

distillation: the plants are put into a large vat and subjected to steam which passes into a still where it condenses. The liquid collected is the plant's essential oil. It is much more concentrated than the original plant (as much as 200 times more!) Essential oils can kill germs and fungus infections, relieve pain, cure inflammation; they can be soothing or astringent, treat indigestion or act as stimulants. There are some that have sedative, hypnotic, antidepressant or relaxing properties.

Concentrate on the knotty areas

Massage is the best method of using essential oils to get rid of stress. One reason is that this removes all risk of poisoning: when taken internally, essential oils need to be very carefully managed indeed. Another is that the relaxing effects of the massage enhance those produced by the oil itself.

To prepare a massage oil: take 200 ml (7 fl oz) of a base oil (grape seed, apricot stone, jojoba, avocado, hazelnut etc) and add 2 teaspoons of mixed essential oils. Use two or three tablespoons of this mixture for each massage. Concentrate on the parts of the body that get particularly knotted (shoulders, nape, back) and finish by massaging the whole body.

> To reduce anxiety: lemon balm, patchouli, clary sage.
> To combat depression: bergamot orange, rose, jasmine, sandalwood.

KEY FACTS

* Essential oils are the concentrated form of plants, with very potent qualities.

* They have, among others, calming, relaxing, hypnotic or antidepressive effects.

* To combat stress, use them for massage.

20 give yourself a boost with wheatgerm

To deal with stress our nervous system needs B vitamins. When the going gets tough, give your body a boost by taking supplements of wheatgerm, the best nourishment nature can provide.

Flour, bran and germ. Wheat provides us with a rich store of anti-stress vitamins in the form of its germ, which can be taken as powder, flakes or tablets.

In times of stress we need extra vitamins: wheatgerm contains proteins, lipids and large quantities of vitamins B and E. The B group vitamins are required by the brain and central nervous system. When we are stressed our body needs more of them. However, our diet often lacks B vitamins because they are found in food such as wholemeal cereals, nuts and pulses that contains a large number of calories. A course of wheatgerm fills this gap and there's no danger of putting on weight!

DID YOU KNOW?

> Fresh wheatgerm is simply ground and then made available for sale in the form of flakes or tablets.
> Wheatgerm powder and flakes can be used to season soups, salads and ready-made meals.
> The tablets should be taken morning and evening.

KEY FACTS

* During periods of stress, we need to take vitamin B supplements.

* Wheatgerm is a very good natural source of this vitamin.

* We often don't consume enough B vitamins as they are found in food with a high calorie content.

case study

Me, stressed? Never!

'I'm very, very lucky because I do a job I like. I am a copy editor for several publishers. I work at home and decide my own hours. Sometimes, however, I have to cope with very busy periods which are exhausting. So as not to feel overwhelmed, I make sure I'm ready for them. I regularly play sport, which is relaxing. I take care over what I eat. I don't go short but try to please my appetite and my conscience at the same time! When I go out with friends, I have a great time and don't worry about it but the next day I start to eat healthily again. Also, from time to time I take magnesium and vitamin supplements. I feel I'm in charge, in control of my life, instead of being at the mercy of events. It hasn't always been like this. A few years ago I went through a very bad patch. I was sleeping badly, so I took sleeping pills and became dependant on them. I couldn't bear it. It wasn't easy to sort myself out. I don't want to risk being like that again. Up to now, I've been successful.'

21 »»

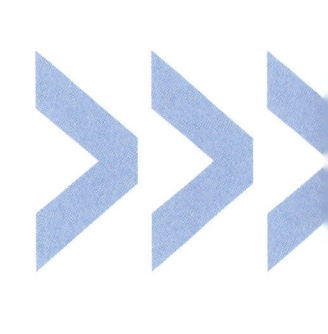

» You're feeling tense, tired, overwhelmed? You really must learn to relax! **If stress is beginning to get to you,** it's because you're letting it.

»»» Learn how to build a wall of serenity around yourself. Practise yoga or qi gong, **learn to do relaxation exercises and meditation,** devise a course of vitamins or floral elixirs for yourself. Let homeopathic medicine calm your anxieties.

»»»»» **All these methods are readily available.** They will help you to naturally regain your inner calm so that you are better able to handle stressful situations.

40
TIPS

21 breathe deeply

We all possess a free, built-in, simple and effective anti-stress mechanism: it is called breathing and all we have to do is learn to follow the proper procedures. So, on your marks, get set…breathe!

A bridge between the body and the mind

Breathing is the only vital function that is both voluntary and involuntary. We continue to breathe while sleeping but can, if we want, speed up or slow down our breathing at will, something it is impossible to do to our heartbeat. Breathing is, therefore, a bridge between the body and the mind, between our unconscious and conscious lives. It is the first thing affected by stressful situations. If we are upset, we get short of breath,

●●● DID YOU KNOW?

> Babies breathe instinctively from the stomach. This is known as abdominal respiration.

> When breath enters the lungs, the diaphragm lowers to allow the chest cavity to open fully. When the lungs are full, the abdominal muscles push the diaphragm upwards and the air is expelled.

we pant and feel a lump in the throat, which makes it difficult for the air to pass through. On the other hand, if we force ourselves to breathe slowly, we become calm once more and the lump disappears.

Learn to breathe

The key to controlled breathing is in exhaling. Concentrate on a brief breath in followed by a long, slow breath out. In this way you will avoid over breathing or hyperventilation, which will make you dizzy and light headed. Swimming underwater really helps breathing technique and gives you back a sense of control. When you are breathing calmly, your heart rate steadies, your blood pressure gets lower and the electrical impulses in your brain get slower. The muscles receive more oxygen, enabling them to get rid of waste products and to relax.

> **To relax and overcome stress, train yourself to breathe from the stomach again.**

KEY FACTS

∗ Breathing is a natural, free and simple way of beating stress.

∗ Emotions disturb our breathing but controlled breathing calms our emotions.

∗ We must get back into the habit of breathing from our stomachs, as babies do spontaneously.

22 learn the best position

The ancient Indian discipline of yoga involves a number of positions, including the dog position, that gently help to rid us of stress. This technique unites body and mind, helping to overcome tension and change the way we look at life. It's an excellent way of escaping when troubles seem all around.

Developing the whole being

In Sanskrit the word 'yoga' means 'union of body and mind'. It originated in the Indus valley more than 2000 years ago and its aim is to develop the whole being. You must concentrate when performing its positions: think of nothing else, breathe deeply and calmly, and let your head go empty.

The dog position stimulates blood circulation, eliminates fatigue and calms the central nervous system.

Drive away tension and regain vitality

• Press your bottom against your heels, letting your toes take the weight, whilst placing your hands and knees on the ground. Lower your chest by letting your hands slide as far forward as possible, whilst keeping your bottom on your heels. Place your forehead on the ground.
• Breathe in and lift yourself up without moving your hands from the ground. Your hips should be in line above your knees. Breathe out and spread out your fingers.
• Breathe in, then, supporting yourself with your hands, lift your hips in order to form an upside down V. Your head should be in a straight line with your spine and your feet supported by your toes. Hold this position for 10 seconds, breathing calmly and deeply.
• Place your heels on the ground and separate your legs slightly. Hold this position for 1 minute, pushing down hard on your spine to achieve the maximum relaxation.

● ● ● DID YOU KNOW?

> Before starting a yoga session, always practise some strong, deep abdominal breathing whilst focusing on how you are breathing. Follow this with some warming and loosening up exercises.
> This prepares both your body and your mind

KEY FACTS

* Yoga is a discipline whose purpose is to develop the whole person.

* It is an excellent method of dealing with stress.

* The dog position calms the central nervous system and improves blood circulation.

23 imagine you're a tree

One of the goals of yoga, as practised in the West, is to teach us to focus our thoughts. This posture is based on physical balance and is wonderful for concentrating the mind.

Bringing physical and mental energy into harmony

The tree position enables you to harmonize physical and mental energy, a harmony often disturbed in times of stress. The position is difficult to hold at first but as it requires concentration, it is perfect for achieving mental relaxation.

Raise your branches to the sky

1 Stand up very straight. Lift your right leg and place your right foot inside your left thigh. Your hips must remain steady. Put your left hand on your hip to keep your balance. Breathe deeply.

2 Look straight ahead of you and stand absolutely still. When you feel perfectly balanced, join your hands together on a level with your solar plexus. Hold the position and breathe calmly for about ten seconds.

3 Lift your arms above your head with fingers interlocked and palms facing upwards like a tree raising its branches towards the sky. Stand still and feel the energy coursing through your body. Do the same exercise with the other leg.

●●● DID YOU KNOW?

There are several forms of yoga.
> Bahkti yoga works upon the emotions;
> Gyana yoga seeks the acquisition of wisdom;
> Raja yoga is mainly concerned with meditation;
> Karma yoga focuses on the repercussions of our actions on our life;
> Hatha yoga is the most physical and it is this that is practised in the West.

KEY FACTS

* The tree position brings physical and mental energy back into harmony.

* Above all, it teaches concentration.

* There are several forms of yoga. Hatha yoga, the most physical, is the form practised in the West.

24 practise the art of the siesta

'Siesta' is not another word for 'laziness' but an excellent way of restoring energy and serenity. Whenever you have the time, use the hour after lunch to recharge your batteries and get rid of tension. And you don't have to live beside the Mediterranean to do this!

The two sleepiest times per day

There are two times when we most need sleep: one is at night when we need it most of all, and the other is in the middle of the day. We do not all react to this second period in the same way. Some people feel neither tired nor sleepy, whilst others mope miserably around until the middle of the afternoon if they cannot rest for half an hour or so.

DID YOU KNOW?

> Numerous scientific studies have been carried out to understand the effects of the siesta but it is potholing that has taught us most.

> The sleep pattern of the first potholers to spend a long time underground without any idea of the passage of time, revealed these two peaks of sleepiness.

If you are in the second group, try to satisfy your need without believing yourself to be lazy. The siesta is an excellent way of achieving relaxation and good health.

Getting rid of tension and tiredness

The siesta does not have to last a long time to revive you. Thirty minutes is enough to give you a boost. In that time you will have got rid of physical and mental tension, and unnecessary tiredness. You will, also, have helped your food to digest and regulated your autonomic nervous system, which controls the body's involuntary activities. In addition, and this is not the least of the advantages, you will have prepared yourself for a good night's sleep. Far from preventing you from sleeping at night, the siesta takes away tiredness and stress, and gets rid of that keyed-up, edgy feeling which disrupts sleep.

> The scientists who observed them also noticed that their day lengthened to about 25 hours instead of the 24 solar hours. Our body doesn't seem perfectly adapted to the planet we live on!

KEY FACTS

* The siesta reflects a physiological need for sleep and is not mere laziness.

* Thirty minutes is enough to revive you.

* It relaxes you, gets rid of tiredness, improves digestion and sets you up for a good night's sleep.

25
breathe a mouthful of pure air

The air we breathe contains not only the oxygen our body needs but also negative ions, which are like invisible vitamins. When we do not get enough of them we become irritable and nervous. Quick, get some pure air!

Positive and negative ions

Ions are oxygen atoms, electrically charged positive or negative. Ions get into the body through the lungs and affect various physiological functions. Positive ions increase the number of chemical substances in the brain that constrict blood vessels. If there are too many of them, they cause migraines, nervousness, insomnia and high blood-pressure. On the other hand, negative ions stimulate the body's metabolism,

DID YOU KNOW?

> Electrical appliances called ionizers produce and circulate negative ions. The efficiency of these machines is as variable as their price.

> They are useful if you live in a very polluted environment where the air outdoors is as poor as indoors.

improve the exchange of ions between liquids and solids, increase mental and physical energy and help to put you in a good mood.

Stand next to waterfalls and fast-flowing streams

Unfortunately, negative ions are much more fragile than positive ones. They are created naturally by the sun's rays or the disintegration of water droplets caused by waterfalls, waves and so on. In the countryside there are as many as 8,000 negative ions per cubic centimetre compared with 3,000 positive ions. After an hour in a confined space the situation is reversed.

To breathe in enough negative ions, take a regular walk in the countryside and air your rooms often. Keeping your windows wide open for just five minutes is enough to clean up the air in a room.

> If you use one of these machines, make sure you don't position it close to a wall: negative ions are destroyed as soon as they encounter a hard surface.

KEY FACTS

* In the air we breathe there are electric particles called ions.

* Positive ions cause nervous tension, whilst negative ions are relaxing and relieve fatigue.

* To breathe in negative ions, walk in the fresh air and air your home thoroughly.

26 try out some oriental dancing

Belly dancing stirs fantasies in men all around the world. Believe it or not, these pelvic undulations are a wonderful source of well-being and relaxation. So get out all those flimsy veils and get moving!

Cradle of life, generator of energy: oriental dancing teaches you to move all the muscles in your body (arms, legs, pelvis, hips, stomach, shoulders) independently of one another. It is a little like what a yogi can accomplish. The attention is fixed on the stomach, our physical and symbolic centre of gravity, the place where life is created and cradled. In Energetic medicine the stomach is considered as the source of vital energies. And, finally of course, it is the centre of sexuality.

Bring repressed emotions to the surface: stress is often caused as much by accumulated tension as by the actual circumstances that are harassing us. Oriental dancing changes our body image and brings repressed emotions to the surface, not forgetting the genuine physical relaxation caused by these broad, supple movements.

● ● ● DID YOU KNOW?

> Oriental dancing originated in ancient Egypt where it was called raks al-sharki.
> Later, in Turkey, in the heart of the Ottoman Empire, it gained so much acclaim that some of the dancers became living legends.

KEY FACTS

* Oriental dancing teaches you how to move all parts of your body.

* The undulating movements cause genuine relaxation.

27 run, jump, move...

There is certainly nothing like sport for getting rid of aggression and tension. However, there are some basic rules of how, when and where to follow, if it is to combat stress.

Listen to your body: this is the only way you can enjoy the physical and psychological benefits of sport. Sporting activity improves breathing, which stress impedes; strengthens the heart, so often overworked when you are stressed; reduces blood pressure; relaxes tense muscles and so on.

The basic rules:
- the ideal programme is 40 minutes, three times per week;
- go gently: don't forget to warm up beforehand and warm down afterwards;
- if you are over 40, haven't taken part in any sport for several years and have health concerns, then it may be a good idea to see your doctor before starting;
- don't forget to drink water during your activity to avoid dehydration.

●●● DID YOU KNOW?

> To reduce stress, doctors advise either endurance sports (walking, jogging, swimming, cycling) or relaxing sports (stretching, gentle gym work), especially if you are doing it in the evening to unwind. It's not the aim to sweat blood!

KEY FACTS

∗ Sport is an excellent way of relieving stress as long as you don't force yourself too hard.

∗ Forty minutes, three times a week is the ideal programme.

∗ Warm up before, drink plenty of water during the activity and warm down afterwards.

28
stretch like a cat

We tend to go tense when trying to cope with stress. Before doing ourselves harm, we should learn to stretch. Stretching is a simple, effective technique that can be done in the gym with a teacher and then by ourselves at home.

Stretch morning and evening

Look at cats: whether small or big, they have a good, long stretch to loosen up their muscles as soon as they wake up. We should copy them! Stretching and loosening exercises are indispensable for people under pressure. They make tension melt away and restore energy. Ideally, do these exercises in the mornings on waking up and in the evenings before going to bed.

Two anti-stress exercises

1 Lie on your back, legs bent towards your chest, hands on your knees. With your hands, slowly draw your knees down onto your chest until you have rolled yourself into a ball.

Tensing your muscles to make them more relaxed

The physical relaxation method developed at the beginning of the last century by Edmund Jacobson, an American researcher, is well suited to restless, energetic personalities. It teaches how to achieve a very low level of muscular activity. By means of simple exercises, you will learn to detect and relax muscular tension, so that you work only those muscles required by your daily movements.

For example, lie on your back with your eyes closed. Lift up an arm and make a very tight fist. Concentrate your mind on the muscles which you are tensing. Relax your arm and feel the muscles as they relax.

Feeling the warmth and the weight

Autogenic training was the idea of Johannes Schultz, a German doctor very interested in hypnosis. He undertook to teach his patients how to regain relaxation and calm for themselves. The autogenic technique teaches you to feel the sensations of warmth and weight in your body in order to retrieve the state of mind that caused them. Gradually and with just a little bit of imagination, you can easily and quickly create a mood of serenity.

An example: lie on your back with your eyes closed. Feel calmness entering you and say to yourself, 'I am completely calm'. Then feel your body become warm and say to yourself, 'I feel the heat entering my body'. And so on. Each time you are using a sentence to fix a sensation. With practice, all you will have to do is say the sentence in your head and the state of mind will occur.

> Always do some deep breathing before starting your programme.

KEY FACTS

* Relaxation is the key method of combatting stress.

* Some methods, like Jacobson's, are essentially physical whilst others, like autogenic training, are essentially mental.

* Choose a quiet place to practise in, where you are not likely to be disturbed.

30 listen to the music

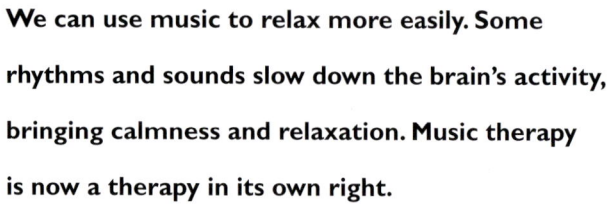

We can use music to relax more easily. Some rhythms and sounds slow down the brain's activity, bringing calmness and relaxation. Music therapy is now a therapy in its own right.

Relaxing the mind, exploring the unconscious

When you listen to music, your body perceives it in the form of vibrations. Your brain deciphers these vibrations and is roused or relaxed, depending on their frequencies. Music can also be used to bring to the surface painful feelings buried deep in the memory. Some psychotherapists even use it to help

●●● DID YOU KNOW?

> Just like humans, animals and plants also like and react to music, as various experiments have proven.

> Research has shown that some dairy cows, for example, give more milk when they listen to Mozart!

explore the unconscious mind in pursuit of hidden desires, ancestral fears, obsessions and so on.

Music is used in Energetic medicine to stimulate positive energies, constructive feelings, imagination and creativity, and to change defensive attitudes caused by the fear of living.

A soundtrack in the background

Although merely listening to soft, calm music helps cause mental relaxation, music therapy itself is a more elaborate matter. It involves a therapist who analyses your needs and tastes in order to compile, with you, a backing track to the therapy which could be relaxation, sophrology, visualization or even massage, depending on the therapist's training. At the end of the session, you are invited to put your experiences into words, to talk about memories that have come to the surface, blockages you have felt, particularly relaxed moments and so on. Whatever the technique, music accompanies and develops the process of inner change.

> Experiments have been performed that show that houseplants appear to grow better when classical music is played nearby. Talking to your plants is recommended by some – why not try singing!

KEY FACTS

* The body perceives music in the form of vibrations, some of which slow down the brain's pattern of activities.

* Music therapy is a genuine form of therapy.

* It combines listening to music with other techniques (sophrology, visualization, massage etc.).

31 learn to meditate

To deal with stress, you need to be in control mentally. However, if you keep on turning your problems over and over in your mind, you end up not knowing what you want or who you are. Meditation enables you to regain a state of inner calm.

Bringing our shattered minds back together again

When it is too violent or prolonged, stress shatters us and scatters the pieces. We feel completely 'untogether' and unable to face up to our circumstances and problems. To 'put the pieces back together again', oriental religions use meditation.

●●● DID YOU KNOW?

> Initially, these exercises seem impossible to our western minds. All it needs are some patience and perseverance.

> That is why it is very helpful to learn a specific technique from a master in, for example, a Zen dojo, a Tibetan monastery or Indian cultural centre.

Indian, Tibetan, Japanese (See Tip 32) forms of Buddhism, Hinduism and Taoism all have their own particular techniques but these techniques also have a lot in common. Above all, they have the same aim: to stop you obsessing about your problems and instead, to empty your mind so that you understand things more clearly.

Position, respiration, concentration

First of all, position: you must always adopt a specific position and then keep still. Usually it is a sitting position. If you were lying down you would be liable to fall asleep, which is not the object of the exercise. The purpose is, in fact, to silence the body, to liberate it from certain demands, particularly that of having to adapt to standing upright, and to let the mind work in peace.

Next, respiration: by concentrating on your breathing, you can slow it right down, relaxing body and mind. Once this state of relaxation has been achieved, concentration enables you to free your mind of destructive thoughts. Should a thought intrude, start breathing slowly again and it will melt away.

Finally, concentration: to help the mind stay silent, certain techniques use mantras. These are words or short phrases, which are repeated over and over again to occupy the mind and prevent it from thinking any thought that would start it churning over again.

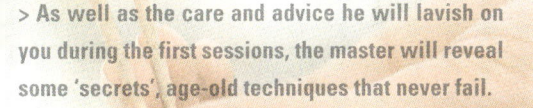

> As well as the care and advice he will lavish on you during the first sessions, the master will reveal some 'secrets', age-old techniques that never fail.

KEY FACTS

* To regain strength and serenity, learn to meditate.

* All eastern philosophies and religions have their own methods.

* The three main rules are: position, respiration and concentration.

32 try zen

Zen is a Japanese and essentially Buddhist philosophy. It is based upon zazen, meditation in a seated position. It seems simple but is not necessarily easy! However, with a little patience, you can achieve peace and serenity.

The principle...

The master Deshimaru, the Japanese sage who introduced this discipline to the West, used to say, 'To know the essence of Zen, practise zazen.' The daily practice of breathing, concentration and meditation leads to the creation of inner being and the profound transformation of the individual disturbed by the demands and obsessions of the ego.

... and the posture

Sit with legs crossed, knees on the ground, right foot on your left thigh and left foot on the cushion. Keep your back very straight, eyes half-closed and chin pressed in, as if you want to push against the sky with the top of your skull. Put your hands together in front of your navel with palms facing upward. Put your thumbs together to form a circle. And that's all! Then breathe calmly and deeply, concentrating on breathing out, and trying not to think of anything. That is the most difficult part. Deshimaru used to say, 'You must let your thoughts pass gently by like clouds in the sky. Don't think about life, be life!'

● ● ● DID YOU KNOW?

> Research has shown that the practice of zazen slows the brain's activity (the outer layer of the brain is at rest but the brain is still alert), increases blood flow (the tissues receive more oxygen) and improves the working of the central nervous system.

> A marked reduction of nervousness and anxiety, and improvement of alertness and memory were also noted, as was a fall in blood-pressure among high blood-pressure sufferers.

> Not to mention the long-term effect – a greater ability to deal with the uncertainties of life!

KEY FACTS

* Zen is a Japanese, essentially Buddhist, philosophy.

* It is based upon silent, seated meditation called zazen.

* Zazen calms, relaxes and improves alertness and memory.

33 listen to the sound of silence

What better way to relax than to make our inner self silent? Unfortunately, we are so used to noise that silence frightens us. We must learn to treat it as a friend again, immediately!

Inner silence leads to serenity: inner silence is an open door leading to serenity. Many opinion polls have shown that noise is the form of pollution most people complain about. Because we are so bombarded with sounds, we lose the habit of listening to our own silence. It is easy enough to reduce the noise we make (not talking for talking's sake, controlling the noise we generate around us) but it is much harder to achieve inner silence.

There is one way of managing it: make that chatterbox inside our heads shut up! Here is a ten-minute exercise to do each day:
- sit comfortably in a quiet place, back and head straight, shoulders relaxed;
- breathe deeply;
- let your thoughts swirl past you without trying to catch them and concentrate on the noises within, such as your breath coming in and going out and your heart beating.

●●● DID YOU KNOW?

> This exercise revives the desire for silence, as we come to realize the noise we have inside us.
> Gradually however, our thoughts subside and we understand that the sounds we now hear inside our body are the rhythms of our life and the signs of our vital energy.

KEY FACTS

* Achieving inner silence is a source of relaxation and serenity.

* To silence your thoughts, concentrate your mind on the sounds of your body.

34 breathe through your skull

Yes, the skull breathes! And when its delicate movements are obstructed we become irritable and tired. On the other hand, when it moves freely again we can once more cope calmly with our worries.

Very gentle manipulation: osteopathy is a manual technique. It is based upon a simple idea: we are made up of three basic, continually interacting parts, the framework of muscles and bones, the internal organs and the mind. By means of very gentle manipulative movements, the osteopath can restore the balance between them.

The skull breathes! Some osteopaths concentrate their work on the skull. It is thought that the cranial bones move imperceptibly as if they are breathing. Osteopaths call this the 'primary respiratory movement'. These tiny movements can be impeded or even prevented with the result that we feel unhappy, tired, irritable and nervous. Stress can cause these blockages. To feel calm again, we need to allow the skull to breathe once more.

DID YOU KNOW?

> During labour a baby's head is often squeezed, which could upset the movements of the cranial bones.
> This is why cranial osteopaths work mainly with young children, even babies.

KEY FACTS

* Osteopathy is a therapy, which restores the balance of the whole person by means of gentle manipulative movements.

* Cranial osteopathy seeks to restore the tiny movements of our cranial bones.

* This treatment is also given to babies.

35 be a tiger in spring

In Chinese medicine it is thought that anxiety is caused by a disturbance in the flow of energy from the liver. To relieve the anxiety, the normal flow must be restored. Qi gong, the gymnastics of the Chinese energy system, achieves this.

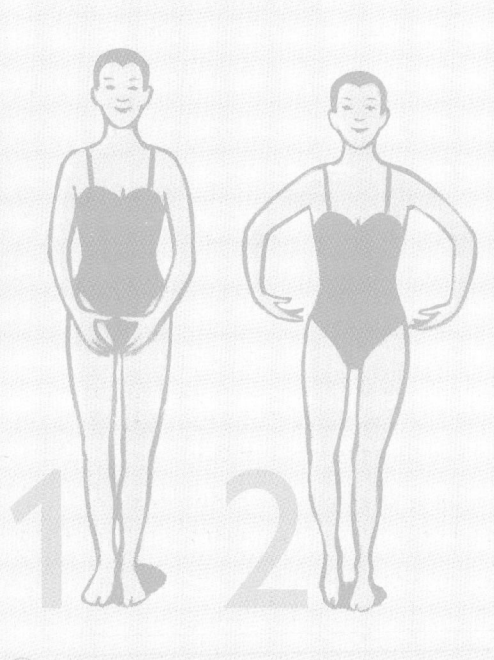

When the energy flow from the liver is disturbed

According to Chinese medicine, the life within us is sustained by vital energy which circulates along channels called meridians. Everything is fine if this circulation flows normally but imbalances occur if there is a disturbance. One of these meridians is linked to the liver. It crosses the whole body from the big toe to the forehead. Along its path it performs various functions, some of which affect psychological and nervous balance. When the flow of energy is too strong in the liver meridian we become impatient, angry, nervous and irritable. When it is too weak we are timid and subject to fears, phobias and inhibitions.

Regulating energy with Qi gong

To correct these imbalances of energy the Chinese use diet, plants, acupuncture and Qi gong exercises. The tiger posture

is a wonderful way of regulating energy from the liver:
1 Stand with your feet slightly apart, arms down in a circle in front of you and bend your knees.
2 Put more of your weight on your right leg, which should now be a little more bent than the left one. Spread your arms but keep them rounded. Your fingers should be like claws held ready to attack, your eyes wide open and the look on your face ferocious.
3 Slowly stretch your left leg whilst spreading your arms right out. Breathe naturally and calmly. Concentrate your mind on the centre of your palms for at least one minute before relaxing.

DID YOU KNOW?

> Traditional Chinese medicine maintains that spring is the time when you should imitate the tiger in order to stimulate energy from the liver.
> Each meridian is associated with a major organ and each organ is associated with one of the seasons. Spring is the season of the liver.
> Exercises to regulate energy will be most effective during the Spring season.

KEY FACTS

* Practitioners of Chinese medicine believe that nervousness and anxiety are caused by a disturbance in the liver meridian.

* To regulate the circulation of energy in this meridian, perform Qi gong exercises.

* The tiger position is particularly recommended for this purpose.

36 speak the language of flowers

An English doctor working in the early twentieth century found that subtle flower extracts could be used to treat feelings of uncertainty and other negative emotions. Floral elixirs are particularly suited to help us cope with the trials and tribulations of modern society.

Flowers and the mind

Very early in his career Dr Edward Bach was convinced that the keys to good health were not to be found in the body but in the mind. To help his patients find emotional harmony, he searched for subtle medicines capable of having a positive effect on our most intimate feelings. His attention naturally turned to flowers which are the final stage of a plant's growth, and therefore, contain all its

●●● DID YOU KNOW?

> To make a floral elixir, pick a flower at dawn and place it in a bowl of pure water exposed to the rays of the sun.

> A subtle alchemy transmits the vital energy of the flower to the water. When the flower has withered collect the water, filter it, mix it with alcohol (50%) and then shake it for a few minutes to help achieve the optimum effect.

vitality. He established links between certain flowers and certain states of mind, and began to use these flowers in a diluted form to cure his patients. Gradually over time all the floral elixirs were discovered.

Four elixirs to combat stress

• If you feel that you are always facing the same problems and are never able to learn from your experiences, take chestnut buds. This elixir increases our ability to adapt and encourages us to live each moment fully.
• If you are pessimistic and incapable of seeing the positive side of things, take gentian. This flower elixir encourages self-confidence, perseverance and determination.
• If you are psychologically and emotionally exhausted, take hornbeam. This elixir restores energy and enthusiasm by changing the way we look at life.
• If you have just suffered an intense shock, take star of Bethlehem. This elixir liberates us from severe stress and also from traumas we cannot forget.

> We now have the concentrated mother-elixir, which is diluted and shaken again to create the pure floral elixir available in health food shops and some pharmacies.
> Take two drops in a glass of spring water.

KEY FACTS

∗ Floral elixirs cause emotional harmony.

∗ Four elixirs are especially suited to relieving the effects of stress.

∗ A floral elixir is made with a flower, a bowl of pure water and the rays of the sun.

37 think homeopathy

Developed by German doctor Samuel Hahnemann at the end of the eighteenth century, homeopathic medicine uses very weak doses to treat patients. It has its critics, but there are many who believe it works. Whoever is right, homeopathy, when practised properly, is neither poisonous or addictive

Tiny but effective doses

Homeopathy uses very tiny doses of animal, vegetable or mineral substances and the fundamental principle of similarity. This principle involves the idea that an infinitesimal amount of a substance will cure illnesses that a normal amount would cause. Take, for example, the onion. When you peel onions, your eyes stream, your nose runs and you sneeze. *Allium cepa*, the homeopathic medicine

●●● DID YOU KNOW?

> Homeopathic doctors are interested in your symptoms and the way in which you talk about your illness.

> That is why they sometimes ask questions that seem unrelated to your problem: are you sensitive to the cold? Do you like sweet or salty food? Are your symptoms worse in the mornings or evenings, indoors or outdoors?

with a base of onion, treats colds which have exactly the same effects on us as peeling onions.

There's a vast range of homeopathic medicines that treat stress-related conditions like anxiety, nervousness, depression, distress and fear.

Some remedies to combat stress

- If you have to put up with repeated or prolonged annoyances, which make you more and more irritable and upset, take *ignatia amara*.
- If you suddenly feel distressed and frightened of death, take *aconite*.
- If you have experienced a sudden shock (the end of a relationship, redundancy), take *arnica*.
- If you feel humiliated but have great difficulty in expressing your anger, take *staphysagria* (stavesacre).
- If you feel completely helpless and tongue-tied when with strangers or superiors, take *ambra grisea* (ambergris).

Take three granules of all these medicines (each with a dilution factor of 12 HC) every morning and evening. If you see no improvement after three weeks consult a homeopathic doctor, who will be able to decide upon just the right remedies for you. Remember that when you are stressed, it is difficult to understand what it is that you really need.

> All these factors will help the doctor choose the medicine exactly suited to your needs from the vast homeopathic range at his or her disposal.

KEY FACTS

∗ Homeopathic medicine uses very tiny doses and is based upon the principle of similarity.

∗ There is a vast range of remedies capable of curing the effects of stress.

∗ Consult a homeopathic doctor to find exactly the right treatment for you.

38
take vitamins!

To cope with stressful situations we need to dig deep into our reserves of vitamins. However, they will not last long and so nor will our resistance. The answer is to take a regular course of vitamins. The four you can bank on to do you some good are vitamins A, B, C and E.

When you're feeling stressed, vitamin pills are the answer

Vitamins and other essential nutriments are quickly used up when we are stressed. Once we run short, symptoms like nervousness, anxiety, fear and distress hit us all the harder and our problems seem insurmountable. It is a vicious circle. To escape from it, we need to rebuild our stock of essential nutriments. A course of vitamin supplements one month out of every three is a good

● ● ● DID YOU KNOW?

> Stress increases the production of free radicals in the body. These radicals speed up the ageing process in all tissues.
> To curb this harmful process, make sure you have enough Vitamins A, C and E, the three anti-free radical vitamins.

> So regularly take supplements of beta-carotene (provitamin A), vitamin C (up to 1gm maximum per day) and vitamin E (10mg per day).

way of doing this. Remember that too much vitamin A and D can be harmful. Check your total intake.

Anti-stress vitamins

B1 (thiamin): essential for generating energy from carbohydrates by the cells and for the health of the brain and the peripheral nerves. Requirements are increased by drinking alcohol, especially beer. Daily requirement: about 20mg (up to 50mg).

B2 (riboflavin): is a co-enzyme for many reactions in cells. It is not destroyed by cooking but is destroyed by sunlight. Daily requirement: about 5mg.

B5 (pantothenic acid): helps produce adrenaline, the hormone that enables us to react to stressful situations. Daily requirement: 10mg (up to 50mg).

B6 (pyridoxine): produces dopamine and noradrenaline, two neurotransmitters vital for coping with stress, and also improves the production of magnesium (see Tip 3). It is used to combat pre-menstrual tension. Daily requirement: up to a maximum of 100mg.

B12: improves alertness, attentiveness and memory. Daily requirement: 5–30mg (up to 100mg).

KEY FACTS

* Stress depletes our stock of vitamins.

* Take anti-stress vitamin supplements when the pressure is on.

* Be sure to take B group vitamins as well as vitamins A, C and E.

39
let massage improve your life

Our skin is an amazing, but often neglected, source of sensory information. Much of this information can help us to combat stress. It's time to rediscover the calming and stabilizing qualities of massage.

Our skin speaks to us

Our skin is not only an envelope designed to protect our bodies from external dangers but a wonderful means of communication. It possesses millions of sensors which tell us what is hot and what is cold, what is dry and what is wet, what is pleasant and what is painful. It tells us about a lot of other things as well. It makes us aware of the tenderness lavished upon us and the attention paid

● ● ● DID YOU KNOW?

> Touch is the first sense to develop in the foetus. From the very first weeks it receives information about its surroundings through the skin.

> This sense also plays an important role at birth. Research has shown that the tactile stimulation received during childbirth sets in motion certain biological functions, such as the control of the sphincters, and breathing.

to us. This is why some civilizations have turned massage into an art practised daily. In India, for example, whole families, parents and children, husbands and wives, massage each other to improve health, to achieve calm and relaxation, and transmit their affection through touch.

A better relationship with ourselves and with others

We ought to follow the example of the Indians, because stress deprives us of sensations vital to balance and fulfilment. Instead, we go tense and withdraw from other people.

Massage helps us in other ways too, depending on the technique used: for example, it stimulates our vital energy, relaxes bodily tensions and brings buried emotions to the surface. Whatever the technique used however, massage improves our relationship with ourselves, with others and with our surroundings. It is a complete means of improving resistance to stress and our ability to adapt.

> However, in many societies, touching is inevitably linked with an expression of sexuality and is therefore a taboo.

KEY FACTS

* The skin provides us with a wealth of sensations.

* In some societies massage is a part of daily family life.

* Massaging others and being massaged is a source of well-being, relaxation and energy.

40 the finer points of acupuncture

Acupuncture is the branch of Chinese medicine we are most familiar with in the western world. It has proved a very effective way of calming nerves, relieving tension and curing tiredness ... provided you're not afraid of needles!

Removing blockages in the energy flow: for the Chinese, acupuncture is a technique that is only used when preventive therapies have failed. In the West it has been used for several decades to treat symptoms of stress like nervousness, anxiety, insomnia, digestive problems and migraine.

Maintaining the body's energy balance: vital energy circulates in the body along the meridians. By altering these movements, the acupuncturist can disperse an excess of energy or attract energy to places where there is not enough. As far as stress is concerned, the areas needing treatment could be situated in various parts of the body, according to the patient's symptoms, but the top of the skull is the place most often stimulated.

●●● DID YOU KNOW?

> Some people have a panic attack at the sight of needles. If you're like that, acupuncture is not for you.

> On the other hand, if it's the hygienic aspect that concerns you, it isn't a problem any more. Nowadays acupuncturists use sterile needles that are thrown away once they have been used.

KEY FACTS

* Acupuncture regulates the circulation of energy in the body.

* It is an effective way of treating stress symptoms.

* Nowadays acupuncturists use their needles only once.

case study

I keep some time especially for myself

'When I decided to stop working to concentrate on my children, I was pregnant with the youngest. During my last few weeks at work, I felt as if I was about to go on a long holiday. But I soon became disillusioned. Yes, I had more time for my family and the house but I felt imprisoned, cut off from the rest of the world. I got depressed. I was racing around all the time and no longer thought I should let my children have school meals or leave them at the creche. Those were things only working mums did. I lost weight, looked pale and didn't even put on make-up any more. A friend told me I needed to do something about it. I have learned to keep some time especially for myself. Two half-days a week I treat myself to yoga and exercise classes, a massage or a visit to the cinema. I've discovered Chinese medicine and it really does me good. When I feel tired or irritable, I take some herbs or go to the acupuncturist. I've found a balance between responsibilities and enjoyment and, as a result, I am much calmer and more tolerant towards my husband and children!'

41 »»

»» We are sometimes faced with **stressful situations that just go on and on**. We feel powerless to do anything about them. The usual guidelines for a happy, relaxed life are not working anymore.

»»»» When we cannot change the world around us, there is only one thing left to do … **change ourselves**, change our way of seeing things. We make things much worse for ourselves without realizing because we underestimate our own worth. We dare not assert ourselves, and do as we are told without question.

»»»»»» Stop! **It's time you learned to realize your own worth.**

60 TIPS

41 think positive

Positive thinking teaches us not to be afraid of life but to face up to it and to find our hidden strengths. In other words, it is a psychological technique particularly well suited to dealing with the troubles caused by stress.

We are all great

Positive thinking is based on the key premise that we are all great, and gifted with hidden strengths just waiting to be brought to light and used. We are all high-performance cars but go around like old bangers. Many factors limit our horizons and damage our potential, for instance education, commitments or constraints.

● ● ● DID YOU KNOW?

> It was a French pharmacist who created positive thinking at the beginning of the twentieth century.

> Émile Coué noticed that the medicines he dispensed gave better results if he accompanied them with positive advice. He decided to develop this into a technique.

> The principle of Coué's method is that willpower achieves little. It is the imagination that really works. You have to imagine you are successful or cured for positive results. From this comes the famous line, 'Every day in every way, I am getting better.'

Stressful situations make this much worse and we become incapable of doing what we know we can do.
Never mind the hidden potential…!
This is the moment to learn to think positively. Relax and fill your mind with positive, optimistic messages. Eventually your mind will believe them, thus creating the conditions for success.

The present tense affirmative

Positive thinking is taught in various ways. Some techniques just relax you and make you repeat key sentences. Others try to bring harmful emotional tensions to the surface in order to remove them and allow the messages to take root more easily. Here is an example. You are faced with a nerve-wracking situation, for instance a job interview or an exam, and you are afraid of failure. Instead of mulling endlessly over your fears, lie down, close your eyes, breathe calmly and repeat in your head, 'My exam is going very well. Whatever I do, I do successfully.'
There are a few simple rules: the messages must always be in the present tense, contain no negatives and have only one idea per sentence.

KEY FACTS

* We are all much more gifted than we think.

* Positive thinking enables us to prepare better for stressful challenges.

* The key sentences must be in the present tense and contain no negatives.

42
be the star in your own movies

Visualization, the logical follow-up to positive thinking, involves making mental images of scenarios with positive outcomes, in order to fix them in the unconscious mind and make them more effective. There are some simple rules you will need to follow, but you shouldn't find them a problem.

Good for mind and body

Visualization is all about using the imagination for the benefit of mind and body. It involves creating mental images and scenes connected with a problem, in order to resolve the problem. It is valid for all kinds of purposes: healing emotional scars, preparing the way for success or meeting some challenge, achieving calm and serenity, or even for

●●● DID YOU KNOW?

> Visualization can also be carried out with a therapist to bring long-forgotten traumas back into the consciousness and therefore resolve them.

> In this type of case, the session is preceded by a discussion to review the problem and possibly the results of earlier sessions. The scenario is built up by the patient with the guidance of the therapist.

curing illnesses. It is therefore perfectly suited to dealing with stress and all its consequences.

All of us, in fact, visualize quite naturally but we do it the wrong way round – as if we are preparing for the worst. We ought to use the same method to prepare for the best!

The basic rules

Once again the images must be positive, and imagined as if they are actually happening. The session should be relaxed, because being relaxed slows down the brain's activity and creates the best conditions for establishing positive messages. To be really effective, the images must be as fully realized as possible. Don't merely imagine them but live them in your mind: feel the heat of the sun, smell the perfume of flowers, savour the taste of fruit and so on.

> This is then followed by a discussion so that the patient can put the feelings aroused into words and analyse them.

KEY FACTS

* Visualization involves creating a positive imagined situation to solve a real problem.

* To be effective, visualization must take place in a relaxed atmosphere.

* The images must be as positive and real as possible.

43 learn to love yourself

Shakespeare wrote, 'Self-love ... is not so vile a sin as self-neglecting.' 'Self-love' or self-esteem is essential for personal fulfilment. It is the basis of good relations both with yourself and with other people. Valuing yourself as you deserve to be valued is a way of eliminating many causes of stress.

Think of your strong points rather than your weaknesses

Having good self-esteem means being able to judge our worth clearly and without self-deception. This ability is influenced by the way our parents treated us during childhood. If they were encouraging, they will have taught us to see our strong points but if they were always critical, they will have made us too conscious of our weaknesses.

● ● ● DID YOU KNOW?

> Stop comparing yourself to your sister or your brother, your parents or your friends. They are themselves: each has strengths and weaknesses, good points and bad.

> Not being like the people you know does not mean that you are worse than them. Far from it!

> We are all unique and have the right to be loved for ourselves.

Unfortunately, parents often tend to dwell upon our mistakes and failures rather than our successes, so we end up with low self-esteem. As a result, we find it hard to react when our feelings are badly hurt: we accept setbacks and disappointments without protesting and dare not assert ourselves for fear of upsetting others. We feel permanently stressed and worn out physically and mentally. However, this process is not irreversible, no matter how old we are.

How to rebuild self-esteem

We all have weaknesses and strengths. We must try to focus more on our assets in order to make best use of them instead of dwelling on our faults. Try to draw up an honest list of your weak and strong points. To begin with, you will think of many more weaknesses than strengths. That's only to be expected because we live in a society that mistakes self-esteem for vanity. Gradually however, you will think of other strong points. Make a note of them when they occur to you. Every time you have doubts yourself, read that list and it will give you the confidence not to give in.

> It is far better to concentrate on developing the good qualities we do have, rather condemning ourselves for what we lack.

KEY FACTS

* Not liking yourself is the cause of many stressful situations.

* Our level of self-esteem is influenced by what our parents thought of us.

* To rebuild self-esteem we must learn to accept all of ourselves, our weaknesses and also our strengths.

44 stop feeling guilty

Guilt is a dangerous poison. It slowly wears us down, adding the stress of self-reproach to the stresses we experience from the world around us. Although it is worthwhile to examine and judge what we do clearly and honestly, nothing is gained by always feeling guilty about everything. Quite the opposite!

To blame for everything, all the time

Guilty: the verdict that falls on those who have committed a serious offence. Guilty: what we sometimes feel when we have done nothing wrong at all. In the first case, the guilt is productive because it can stop the offence from being repeated. However, in the second case, all it does is poison our lives. A real crime can be confessed, regretted and

● ● ● DID YOU KNOW?

> Guilt starts to grow during childhood. Children tend to feel guilty about what they do not understand, such as the divorce of their parents. Also, family members often unintentionally make remarks that can cause guilt ('You're a liar').

> Some adults feel permanently guilty and have no idea why this is. They take the blame for the faults of others as if they had committed them themselves.

put right, whilst a pervasive feeling of guilt can obsess us and prevent us from ever feeling at peace.

Replace guilt with responsibility

To escape from this obsession, we must try to replace a feeling of guilt with one of responsibility. It is not easy but it works. If guilt paralyses and ties us to what we have done, responsibility motivates and offers a different future. When we firmly accept responsibility for our actions we can understand their consequences, judge them and, if necessary, correct them. Above all, we can learn not to make the same mistakes again. Gradually we evolve instead of remaining trapped in stressful situations. We make progress, moving forwards instead of backwards.

> In cases like these, it might be advisable to get the help of a psychotherapist to identify the cause and resolve the condition.

KEY FACTS

* Guilt is negative. It is much better to replace it with the feeling of responsibility.

* The feeling of guilt starts to grow during childhood.

* When it takes too strong a hold, it might be advisable to consult a psychotherapist.

45
set yourself reasonable targets

To arrive at our destination, there needs to be a road that takes us there. Sometimes we set ourselves totally unrealistic targets and then feel despondent when we do not live up to them. We need to get out of this vicious circle ... and quickly!

Trying to live up to a mistaken image of ourselves

To achieve what we set out to do, our aims must be realistic. That is obvious, but sometimes, without realizing it, we set ourselves unachievable goals. It is not hard to see why. We sometimes find it difficult to correctly judge both the difficulties that confront us and our ability to deal with them. We are inclined to think we are stronger, more beautiful and

●●● DID YOU KNOW?

> There is a Chinese proverb that says, 'A journey of a thousand leagues begins with one step.' In the West we say, 'One step at a time.'

> The two sayings are expressing the same idea: if we have a long way to go, we must go steadily forward without demanding too much of ourselves and without taking too much out of ourselves.

more intelligent than we actually are. By striving to satisfy this mistaken image of ourselves, we get sucked into a spiral of failure. The harder our aims are to achieve and the more difficulties and failures we experience, so the more stressed and dissatisfied with ourselves we become.

New and simple measures

There are some simple measures you can take to change all this. For example:
- allow yourself more time for your projects;
- if you haven't been able to solve a problem, make a note of your difficulties and ask friends and family to help you;
- make a list of what you want to do every day to get an overview instead of weighing yourself down with a lot of different, incompatible tasks.

This will help you plan more sensibly and improve your ability to judge what is, and what is not, reasonable.

> We must also learn to forget for a while how far we still have to go, so we can feel satisfied with the small distance we have already covered. This is the only way to have the courage to carry on.

KEY FACTS

* To be achievable, our aims must be realistic.

* If we have a mistaken idea of what we are capable, we sometimes get sucked into a spiral of failure.

* To avoid this, we need to change our approach by giving ourselves more time, getting help and listing our daily tasks.

46 take your time

The more rushed we are, the more time we must allow ourselves. It sounds self-contradictory but rushing is a major source of stress. Learning to manage our time is a much better idea.

Get time under control

It is when we are under pressure that we feel most short of time. We seem to chase after time without ever catching it but it can become our friend and ally. All we need to do is get it under control. Time is entirely subjective: it depends on what we do and how we do it. Getting it on our side opens up a new, better way of life because it will bring a lot of other improvements with it too.

● ● ● DID YOU KNOW?

> Learning to unplug your telephone may seem a small point, but it is always when you are most under pressure or have urgent work to finish off that it never stops ringing.

> Your priority is to finish what you have started, so turn off your mobile, switch on your answerphone and unplug your landline.

Make lists, organize, plan

Here are a few ideas to help you try to avoid running around in ever-decreasing circles:
- start the day by making a complete list of everything you need to do and think about. This will save you from worrying in case you miss something and it will also help you to plan your jobs.
- organize your time so that you do the most important things first. Then, if you don't manage to do everything, you will at least have done all the things that really matter.
- take account of your biological clock when planning your day. If you feel tired after lunch, don't plan anything important for that time.
- give yourself a small slot in the day when nothing is scheduled. This will come in handy if you are running late or if something unforeseen happens. Otherwise, you can simply enjoy it.
- don't let yourself be overwhelmed by other people needing help. It's good to help but there's no point in running yourself ragged. Dare to say 'No'!

> You will not be out of contact with the outside world for long but, for now, just let it wait!

KEY FACTS

* When we are stressed we never have enough time. This is the moment to learn time management.

* Managing time means planning and organizing but also treating yourself to some 'windows' for relaxation or dealing with the unforeseen.

* Learn to unplug or switch off your phone from time to time!

47 accept your failures

Our mistakes are valuable. We can learn from them and do better next time. We must try not to forget them but instead value them for what they can teach us.

An idealized image of ourselves

What could be more stressful than failure? We feel like wiping the slate clean and starting all over again. We are disappointed and, if it is a big failure, even ashamed or humiliated. And yet, it is the sum of our failures that has made us what we are because we learn most of life's lessons from them, provided we accept them.

••• DID YOU KNOW?

> Nobody can be expected to be perfect! We sometimes confuse the desire for improvement with the desire for perfection.

> Of course, we have to want to do better or we will never improve. 'Where there's a will, there's a way.'

What prevents us accepting them is our desire to be perfect. Because we find it hard to like ourselves as we really are, we project an idealized image of ourselves which we try to live up to. Consequently, although we consider it perfectly normal for other people to fail, it is totally unacceptable if we do. An inverted and stressful form of pride!

Change what you say to yourself

Above all, you need to change what you say to yourself:
- instead of saying, 'I ought never to have done that', say, 'Next time I'll do it differently';
- rather than repeating to yourself, 'I'm useless, worthless, I never do anything well', admit, 'I did my best, the next time I'll do it differently';
- instead of thinking, 'I'll never risk making a mistake again', dare to think, 'OK I got it wrong but I know why and I'll put it right'.

> However, 'wanting to do better' means 'striving towards', not 'having absolutely to succeed'. This sense of obligation only makes us feel worse about ourselves when we do not succeed immediately.

KEY FACTS

* To develop and learn from life, we must accept our mistakes.

* We can learn a lot from our failures and errors.

* To be able to accept our failures, we must stop being furious with ourselves when we do something wrong.

48 choose your friends carefully

Some people help and support us, whilst others criticize us whatever we do. We have everything to gain from being friends with those in the first group. It's a good way of avoiding a lot of stress!

Be brave, run away. Human relationships are complicated affairs and so are our friendships. Sometimes we do all we can, whatever the cost, to stay friends with people who hurt us. Insidiously and without appearing to, they undermine all our efforts, ruin all our plans and demoralize us. If we are unable to change them, even after several attempts, we need to muster our courage … and run away!

No hard feelings! There is no point in feeling bitter towards them. In the great majority of cases, people who behave like this have no idea that they are doing any harm. As far as they are concerned, they are doing it 'for our own good'. They do not understand that what they are doing is destructive to their friends and family. That is no reason why we should simply stand and take it though. The best thing to do is to put some distance between them and us.

DID YOU KNOW?

> Some people do not realize that their behaviour is hurtful.
> In such cases it is a good idea to behave in the same way towards them.
> The amazement this causes will, no doubt, help to bring things out into the open.

KEY FACTS

* Some people systematically undermine all your efforts.
* When all your efforts to change them fail, stay away from them!

49 don't be mean with compliments

Almost all of us tend not to say aloud the admiration we feel inside. However, our compliments will spark off kind and supportive words from the people we praise.

Confidence, affection and support: we all need reassurance from our nearest and dearest now and again. Words of support, words of affection, compliments can do us more good than anything else. Hearing that other people have confidence in us makes us feel much better about our doubts and weaknesses. The best method of getting compliments is to give them.

Mean what you say and say what you mean: you should not pay compliments merely in the hope of getting them back from people who might feel they have to 'repay' you. Be sincere. Get into the habit of saying aloud all the kind things you are thinking. For one thing, this will please your friends and family which is always nice, and secondly, it will create a climate of trust which will make them feel able to say what they feel.

> If you are shy and dare not put into words all the kind things you feel, express them through presents and acts of thoughtfulness.

> Send flowers, leave notes, take chocolates to the office. Your actions will speak for you!

KEY FACTS

* We all need the reassurance that comes from words of support and affection.

* To receive such messages, we must give them.

* This will give others the confidence to do the same for us.

50
learn to communicate better

We would avoid a lot of pointless stress if we were always correctly understood. Unfortunately however, misunderstandings are all too commonplace. So let's improve both our verbal and non-verbal means of communication.

Badly expressed and misunderstood messages

In the stress management courses run by companies one of the subjects most frequently dealt with is communication. A lot of tension and conflict is caused by badly expressed or badly understood messages and instructions. Nowadays some very detailed techniques exist, in particular Neuro-Linguistic Programming

● ● ● DID YOU KNOW?

> We communicate not only with words and intonations but also with gestures. Research has shown that our body movements contribute more to the understanding of a message than the words themselves.

> We can easily select the words we want to use but it is harder to keep a check on our attitudes and body language.

(NLP), that teach us how to know ourselves better in order to make ourselves better understood. NPL was developed in the 1970s by two Americans, Richard Bandler and John Grindler. The first was a computer programmer, the second a linguist, and both were deeply interested in psychotherapy. Their programme is designed to enable us to understand our patterns of behaviour and the means we use to communicate. Once this has been achieved, it becomes easier to modify both how we communicate and how we behave with others.

Choose the right moment and the right method

You can also improve the way you communicate with the people around you by following these simple pieces of advice:

- **choose the right moment:** the person you are contacting, like everyone else, has a clearer mind in the morning than in the evening after a day's work;
- **the medium used:** if the person you are dealing with is forgetful, write to him/her;
- **the method:** avoid giving too much information all at once. Instead, select one point and repeat it (but not so often that it becomes irritating) until it is understood. You will then be able to move on to the next point.

Above all, don't forget that you are only responsible for one half of the act of communication (the formulation of the message). The other half (the receipt of the message) depends on your correspondent. And you can't do anything about that half!

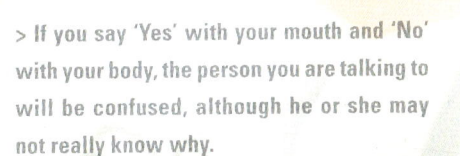

> If you say 'Yes' with your mouth and 'No' with your body, the person you are talking to will be confused, although he or she may not really know why.

KEY FACTS

* Many stressful situations are the end result of bad communication.

* Think carefully about when and how you communicate your message.

51 don't let yourself be manipulated

Manipulators are everywhere. Using charm or bullying, intelligence or shyness, they are able to get what they want from us, even against our will. We can, however, protect ourselves against this very widespread form of emotional stress.

DID YOU KNOW?
> Do you know a manipulator? If so, try not to feel hostile towards him/her.

> If they cannot stop themselves from behaving in such a pathological way, it is probably because they are suffering much more, both emotionally and psychologically, than they appear to be.

> Above all else, protect yourself.

Firstly, identify the manipulators…

We have all met them, both in the family and at work. Sometimes they are charming, sometimes they make us feel guilty and sometimes they are bad-tempered. Their aim is always to get what they want without caring about anyone else. They are often capable of making us behave so out of character that we sink into despair, fear and depression without really knowing why.

To protect ourselves from manipulators we must first be able to identify them. Here are a few clues: they make others feel guilty; they load their own responsibilities onto other people; their answers to questions are vague; they change their opinions whenever it suits them; they cloak their demands in the form of logical reasoning; they make others feel small without seeming to and make themselves look like victims to arouse compassion and pity.

…in order to be able to protect yourselves from them.

To protect yourself, you must first stop hoping that one day you will be able to communicate normally with them. You must not, above all, expect a manipulator to change unless he/she undertakes a course of therapy.

The psychologist Isabelle Nazare-Aga suggests that 'keeping them in the dark' is the best strategy: never justify yourself, never respond directly to their comments and hide your anxiety as much as you can. To help yourself, use ready-made phrases that turn the conversation back round to him/her: 'If that's what you think', 'Each one to his own taste', 'It's possible to see things that way' and so on. Also, be more self-assertive: the more sure you are of yourself, your wishes and your opinions, the less of a hold the manipulator will have over you.

Finally, avoid all difficult situations as soon as you realize what is going on: don't make any more efforts, don't respond to bullying demands, even though it may not be easy.

KEY FACTS

* Manipulators are capable of getting all they want from us.

* To protect ourselves from them, we must first learn to identify them.

* Then we should defend ourselves by 'keeping them in the dark'.

52 express your emotions

Some people are very good at spontaneously expressing their joy and anger, their sadness and their fear. Others find it much more difficult. However, repressed emotions eventually swell up inside us causing permanent, and often very damaging, stress.

Identify, channel and express

Psychologists have identified six fundamental emotions that all human beings share, whatever society they belong to: joy, disgust, surprise, sadness, anger and fear. These affect our psychological state and reflect our relationship with the world and the life we lead. Everyone feels emotions, although their intensity differs from individual to individual:

●●● DID YOU KNOW?

> Stress specialists tend to classify individuals into three categories according to their behaviour, particularly their ability or failure to express emotions.

> Type A individuals are always in a hurry and tense. They demand a lot from themselves and others. They are always ready to suppress emotions that do not help them achieve their goals.

> Type B personalities are more relaxed and less obsessed with success. They find it easier to express their feelings.

some people are overwhelmed by them, whilst others are scarcely affected.
Whether we belong to the first group or the second, we must learn to identify, channel and express what we feel. Our psychological and physical well-being depends upon it. Repressed emotions will eventually demoralize us and then attack our body. Many psychomatic illnesses are due to long years of stifling our emotions.

Don't go from one extreme to the other

Any method that enables you to express your emotions is a good one, provided it does not lead you from one extreme to the other. There is no point in replacing total silence about your feelings with fierce emotional outbursts directed at the people you know. Effective emotional expression must release your inner tensions (good or bad, pleasant or unpleasant) at the same time as improving your communication with those around you, so that there are fewer misunderstandings and quarrels.

The creative arts are an excellent way of learning to express your emotions: paint, sing, make clay sculptures, dance, talk to the trees in the wood. It's up to you to find what works for you!

> Type C personalities are totally introverted and inhibited and seldom, if ever, talk about their feelings.
> Types A and C are the most liable to suffer from the negative effects of stress, particularly the physical ones.

KEY FACTS

* There are six basic emotions experienced by all human beings.

* Different individuals experience these emotions to different degrees.

* Expressing them in a controlled, measured way removes tension and improves relationships with other people.

53
dare to let go

'Letting go' is a notion dear to eastern societies. Indian and Chinese philosophies advocate living in the 'here and now' without thinking about the past or future. This is not easy for westerners to do but it is a very good way to relieve unnecessary stress!

Leave the past behind

Each time we take a breath we breathe air into our lungs, release it and then breathe in again. Imagine what would happen if we refused to let go of the air trapped inside us. We would not be able to take in the next mouthful of oxygen and would die of suffocation.

Yet, that is what we regularly do by refusing to 'let go' of worries, problems, grievances and the desire for revenge.

●●● DID YOU KNOW?

> Nothing around us stays the same, everything is in a permanent state of flux. The mountains even, which seem so unchangeable, are daily being altered by erosion.

> Our worries and misfortunes are just as subject to change.

> There is, however, no reason to feel helpless. We must welcome all the gifts that life has in store for us with open arms.

Once a situation is over, resolved either well or badly, it belongs to the past. All the time we remain tied to it by constantly thinking about it, it stays alive within us and we deprive ourselves of the other adventures life has in store.

Accepting, forgiving, understanding

It is not easy to behave as wisely as that but with a little time and perseverance, everyone can manage to. 'Letting go' does not mean 'forgetting' but 'accepting', 'forgiving' and 'understanding'. Here are some ideas to try:
- let go of your negative feelings: you still feel them but they are not the essential 'you'. They will fade away like autumn mist;
- learn to be more objective: if you don't assume that everything you want will necessarily come true, the world will not seem to collapse when you are sometimes disappointed;
- try to think about what you have instead of concentrating on what you haven't got;
- do your best to think about all the good things life has to offer at every moment: by dwelling on the past and wondering about the future, we forget to enjoy the present to the full.

KEY FACTS

∗ We must let go of past events and emotions if we are to live life to the full.

∗ Concentrate on the present: it has plenty to offer us.

∗ Everything changes, nothing lasts for ever, not even our problems and unhappiness!

54 spare some time for yourself

Enjoying yourself is one of the very best ways of combatting stress. Don't forget to spare a little time to treat yourself to those simple little pleasures that nobody else can offer you. Just a few minutes can sometimes alter the whole complexion of a day.

DID YOU KNOW?

> Sparing some time for yourself and spoiling yourself with little pleasures are part of a treatment prescribed by a doctor.

> Dr Carl Simonton, an American cancer specialist, adds a list of treats to his prescriptions. He asks his patients to write a list of things they enjoy, little things like a chocolate ice cream, or big things like a

Escape by doing something enjoyable

It is precisely when we are under pressure, overworked, overwhelmed and with far too much on our mind that we need to spare some time for ourselves. Time to do what? That depends on the individual. What matters is that we should not spend time mulling over our problems but escape them by doing something we enjoy.

There are several benefits from doing this. Firstly, relaxation: merely thinking of something else calms us down. In addition, giving ourselves a break is sometimes enough to change the way we look at things. The next day we see the situation more clearly and the solution springs, of its own accord, out of our relaxed mind.

Do some gardening or cooking or go for a stroll

Escape by doing whatever you enjoy doing: shopping with friends, gardening, DIY, sewing, drawing, walking, going to the cinema, listening to music, enjoying a cup of tea and cake. It's up to you!
Ideally, however, try and do something which allows you to express your repressed emotions (pottery or painting) or which enables you to create something you can later admire or savour (gardening or cooking).

boat trip around the world, all in no particular order. Each day they are required to enjoy one of them. It's doctor's orders!

KEY FACTS

* It is precisely when you are stressed that you should make some time for yourself.

* Gardening, DIY, drawing… do whatever you enjoy.

* Ideally, use the time to express your emotions or exercise a creative talent.

55 let the words flow from your pen

Some people, when confronted by a blank page, can write reams and reams, whilst others struggle to write anything at all. Whichever group we belong to, what we produce on the page speaks volumes.

Write a letter and… then burn it. Writing is not something for great authors only! We can all write in order to understand ourselves better and express, in a different way, the tensions we feel. For example, to get things out into the open, you are intending to speak to someone about the serious grievances he/she has caused you. To avoid an angry quarrel, start by writing a letter explaining why you feel as you do. Be as aggressive as you like. Re-read the letter, correct it and when you are completely satisfied with it, burn it! You will approach the meeting in a much calmer, more relaxed state of mind.

Write with your left hand: people on some personal development courses are asked to write with their non-writing hand. This exercise enables them to remember what it was like to be a child and to express emotions repressed since the advent of adulthood.

DID YOU KNOW?

> The ultimate exercise is to write with both hands at once. With your writing hand, you express conscious thoughts and with your non-writing hand, you tend to reveal what is usually suppressed. This may help to get you out of awkward situations.

KEY FACTS

* Put all your anger into a letter, then burn it.

* Bring suppressed emotions to the surface by writing with your non-writing hand.

56 play several roles

We often play roles in real life (mother or father, good employer or good employee) without realizing what we are doing. However, we can actually use acting as a way of coming to terms with our emotions.

Putting ourselves in someone else's shoes: the therapeutic use of drama is not something new. As far as dealing with stress is concerned, putting ourselves in someone else's shoes can allow us to understand different points of view and help us to modify our own view of events. It can also sometimes calm anger, get rid of inner tensions and soothe disturbed emotions.

Expressing repressed emotions: using the medium of drama has two psychological benefits. When we play a role, we can express emotions that would otherwise be repressed. We can let our anger explode or say what we really feel to the person opposite us playing the part of our mother, teenage son or head of department. Then, we can change places and reverse the roles.

DID YOU KNOW?

> Psychodrama is a group therapy that uses the medium of drama. It is carefully supervised and guided.

> The therapist directs the sessions and steps in when emotions become too strong. He then helps the participants to accept their emotions in order to understand and take charge of them.

KEY FACTS

* When we play a role, we feel able to express buried emotions.

* We can also take the role of the other person in order to understand his/her point of view better.

* Psychodrama is group therapy.

57 discover the child within you

Deep inner tensions, particularly those that connect the child we were with the adult we have become, keep us feeling stressed. We need to bring these two back into harmony immediately.

Your inner child deserves attention

Adults rarely give expression to the child inside themselves. We gagged, even forgot all about, the child when we put on our solemn adult clothes. Yet the child still lives on deep inside us.

This child has suffered to a greater or lesser extent, depending on our personal history. Our parents' concern for conformity has, in varying degrees, stifled him/her but it is still worth our while to

● ● ● DID YOU KNOW?

> **Making friends** with the inner child is also genuinely therapeutic. The wounds we suffered in childhood are sometimes still there inside us. It is the child who feels the pain. He/she needs to be comforted to become happy again.

> **Try this exercise.** Relax and visualize the child you were. Take him/her in your adult's arms and rock him/her whilst murmuring words of consolation and comfort.

take notice of the child. Our sense of humour and lightheartedness depend upon it as well as our resistance to stress. Being able to laugh at things is often the best way of defending ourselves against tension and pain. Making friends with the child we once were enables us not only to cure these problems, but also to enjoy life and feel untroubled once again.

Play just like you did when you were small!

To do this, we must learn to play again. When we were children, we loved doing that! Games were the basis of our relationship with the world. We can play through writing and acting (See 56). We can also paint and make sculptures and, just like children, not worry about the result. We can use our body to dance and move or we can play a musical instrument we have never played before. Any kind of game is good as long as it allows us to escape from our inhibitions. It is a bit embarrassing to begin with but we soon get used to it, because the child inside us is having such a good time.

KEY FACTS

* The child we were is still there inside us.

* We must make friends with this child to regain peace and the joy of living.

* Learn to play again. This is what makes our inner child most happy.

58 get into training

Many people suffer from panic attacks. They paralyse us and make us feel helpless. To ensure you don't suffer from a last minute attack, you need to prepare for your big moments. Homeopathy, visualization and breathing exercises can all help you.

What a nightmare!

Panic is a nightmare for those who experience it regularly. When they are standing alone in front of the mirror, they can do anything: ask for a colossal pay rise from their boss, announce to their partner they are going to leave, make a brilliant speech in front of a thousand people and so on. However, when they are actually doing it, everything goes wrong: they cannot catch their breath, their mind is completely empty and their

●●● DID YOU KNOW?

> There is a homeopathic medicine that is excellent for avoiding panic attacks.

> A week before the big day try taking a dose of *Gelsemium* (dilution factor 15 C).

forehead is beaded with sweat. It is like falling into a black hole. They leave disappointed at not having done what they set out to do, ashamed at having been so useless and humiliated by their failure.

Yet no one need be doomed to panic attacks for ever. To avoid them, you must prepare yourself psychologically and physically for your big moments, just like a top sportsman.

Air and images can keep you calm

First step: breathing. As soon as you feel yourself getting nervous, breathe deeply and slowly (See 21). Remember to focus on the low, slow breath out. Controlling your breathing slows down your heart rate and soon calms you mentally. You can also repeat a key phrase in your head (See 41) whilst breathing. The mere act of breathing deeply every day to the accompaniment of these words will soon keep you calm.

Second step: visualization (See 42). During the days, even weeks, leading up to your big event, visualize perfect success. Imagine every detail: your mastery, the satisfied smiles on the faces around you, the crowd applauding.

> Repeat the dose two days before but don't take any the night before or on the day itself or you might lose your mental sharpness and clarity, two qualities you can't do without on such occasions.

KEY FACTS

* Panic paralyses us and makes us feel completely helpless.

* To avoid it, we need to prepare for our big moments like a star sportsman.

* Deep breathing, visualization and homeopathy are effective methods of overcoming panic.

59 don't be ashamed of running away

Running away is often confused with cowardice. However, when there is no point in fighting, running away is clearly the best strategy and saves us from a lot of unnecessary stress. It also saves us from wasting a lot of psychological and physical energy.

Inhibited action...

The doctor and biologist Henri Laborit studied the behaviour of rats under stress and formulated a theory. When we are in a stressful situation, our body provides us with the choice of two reactions: to stay and fight the aggressor or to run away and hide. Our body has the right biological equipment to react to stress in either way. There is just one problem: there are some situations in

● ● ● DID YOU KNOW?

> Physical distress can result from inhibited action.

> The biological changes in our body, including hormonal secretions, have no outlet and can end up causing sleeplessness, fatigue, stomach pain and migraines. The immune system can also be affected.

> To avoid such repercussions, try at all costs to avoid situations in which you find yourself powerless to respond.

which we can neither fight nor flee. We are now in a state of inhibited action. Whatever we do is no good and pressure mounts. Our biological reactions are pointless. We soon become distressed. If the situation lasts for some time, it can cause depression and then physical illness.

…very much a human problem!

The problem is that we are not rats. As socialized human beings we find ourselves trapped in a state of inhibited action much more often than animals. Social and human relations factors block our instinctive responses: however much we may want to, we cannot just give our unfair boss a black eye or slam the door in his face!

For Henri Laborit, the answer is simple: be prepared to beat a retreat. Dare to run away from situations when this is the only feasible thing to do. Do so without feeling the slightest guilt about any lack of courage, which would only cause more stress anyway. Learn to calmly run away to avoid stress.

KEY FACTS

* When it is pointless to fight, the best thing to do is run away.

* If we can do neither one thing nor the other, we suffer from a state of inhibited action.

* This leads directly to stress, depression and psychosomatic illnesses.

60 words, words, words

When we have no other way of changing a situation, we still have words. In order not to keep our black thoughts, bitterness and worries locked inside us, we need to share them. We must talk about them.

Silence, embarrassment, obstruction: sometimes we cannot talk to people close to us about our problems. An indefinable feeling of embarrassment and unwillingness to speak about our emotions might also be preventing us. It could be that these very factors are the cause of our problems and troubles anyway.

Talking about our tensions, identifying the patterns: if we cannot talk about our feelings to those close to us, we can turn to specialists for help. That's what psychologists, psychotherapists and psychoanalysts are for! The purpose of therapies based on talking is to lead us to express our tensions, to share them and to look for links between them in order to identify possible patterns. When a problem is repeated, when a difficult situation happens regularly, that means the cause is within us.

DID YOU KNOW?

> A psychologist has studied psychology, the science of the mind, and may use treatments such as cognitive behaviour therapy.
> A psychotherapist helps by using approaches involving words, the body, emotions and creativity.
> Psychoanalysts use conversation.
> Psychiatrists are doctors who treat the most serious medical illnesses and specialise in the use of drug treatments.

KEY FACTS

* We are sometimes embarrassed to speak to people close to us.

* If that is so, we can get the help of a therapist.

case study

I learnt to communicate

'For ten years or so I was head of media relations at a small record company. When the label was taken over, my friend and I decided to set up our own communications agency. I was very keen but I began to feel more and more anxious. I felt frightened, I lost sleep, I couldn't do my job and felt useless. Then an article in a magazine opened my eyes for me. It was about stress management, identifying problems, clarifying objectives. I tried to take my problems one by one and analyse them. I realized that I was very frightened of being myself, frightened of being judged, of not doing enough. For years I had done all the extra work other people had loaded on me, I always said 'yes' to everybody. I had psychotherapy for a few months in order to go into it in more depth. That helped me to understand myself better and accept who I am. And then I discovered Neuro-Linguistic Programming which helped me to communicate better with other people, so that I shan't be pushed around again!'

useful addresses

» Acupuncture

British Acupuncture Council
63 Jeddo Road
London W12 9HQ
tel: 020 8735 0400
www.acupuncture.org.uk

British Medical Acupuncture Society
12 Marbury House
Higher Whitley, Warrington
Cheshire WA4 4QW.
tel: 01925 730727

Australian Acupuncture and Chinese Medicine Association
PO Box 5142
West End, Queensland 4101
Australia
www.acupuncture.org.au

» Homeopathy

British Homeopathic Association
Hahnemann House
29 Park Street West
Luton LU1 3BE
tel: 0870 444 3950

The Society of Homeopaths
4a Artizan Road
Northampton NN1 4HU
tel: 01604 621400

Australian Homeopathic Association
PO Box 430, Hastings
Victoria 3915, Australia
www.homeopathyoz.org

» Herbal medicine

British Herbal Medicine Association
Sun House, Church Street
Stroud, Gloucester GL5 1JL
tel: 01453 751389

National Institute of Medical Herbalists
56 Longbrook Street
Exeter, Devon EX4 6AH
tel: 01392 426022

» Massage

British Massage Therapy Council
www.bmtc.co.uk

Association of British Massage Therapists
42 Catharine Street
Cambridge CB1 3AW
tel: 01223 240 815

European Institute of Massage
42 Moreton Street
London SW1V 2PB
tel: 020 7931 9862

» Qi Gong

Qi Gong Association of America
PO Box 252
Lakeland, MN, USA
email: info@nqa.org

World Natural Medicine Foundation
College of Medical Qi Gong
9904 106 Street,
Edmonton AB T5K 1C4
Canada

» Relaxation therapy

British Autogenic Society
The Royal London
Homoeopathic Hospital
Greenwell Street
London W1W 5BP

British Complementary Medicine Association
PO Box 5122
Bournemouth BH8 0WG
tel: 0845 345 5977

» Yoga

The British Wheel of Yoga
25 Jermyn Street
Sleaford, Lincs NG34 7RU
tel: 01529 306 851
www.bwy.org.uk

index

Abdominal breathing 50-51, 52-53
Activities 112-113
Acupuncture 84-85
Addictive psychotropic drugs 27
Alcohol 20-21
Antidepressants 26-27
Anger 44-45, 78-79
Anxiety 44-45
Appetite 22-23
Autogenic training 64-65

Biological rhythms 12-13
Breathing 35, 68-69, 118-119

Calcium 16-17, 40-41
Chinese medicine 74-75
Chronobiology 12-13
Chronopharmacology 12-13
Coffee 20-21
Communication 104-105, 108-109
Concentration 54-55
Coué method 88-89

Depression 44-45
Distress 78-79
Drama therapy 115

Emotions 108-109
Emotional shock 78-79
Essential oils 44-45

Failure 100-101
Floral elixirs 76-77
Food 14-15, 18-19

Guilt 94-95

Herbal medicine 26
Herbal teas 30-31
Homeopathy 26-27, 78-79, 118-119

Irritability 78-79

Laughter 36-37
Lemon balm 30-31
Lunch 14-15

Magnesium 16-17, 40-41
Massage 38-39, 44-45
Medicinal herbs 30-31
Meditation 64-65, 68-69, 70-71
Minerals 18-19, 40-41
Music therapy 66-67

Negative ions 58-59
Neuro-linguistic programming 104-105

Oriental dancing 60
Osteopathy 73

Panic 78-79, 118-119
Phototherapy 42-43
Positive thinking 88-89
Postures 52-53, 54-55, 68-69, 70-71
Potassium 40-41
Psychiatrist 122
Psychoanalyst 122
Psychodrama 115
Psychologist 122

Psychotherapist 122

Qi Gong 74-75

Reflexology 38-39
Relaxation 64-65

Siesta 56-57
Silence 72
Sleep 25, 44-45
Sleeping pills 26-27
Smoking 20-21
Solitude 34
Sport 28-29, 61
Stretching 62-63
Sunlight 42-43
Swimming 32-33

Therapy 115, 116-117, 122
Tiredness 44-45
Touch 82-83
Tranquillizers 26-27

Visualization 90-91, 118-119
Vitamins 18-19, 46-47, 80-81

Walking 28-29
Water 40-41
Wheatgerm 46-47
Winter depression 42-43
Writing 114

Yawning 35
Yoga 52-53, 54-55

Zazen 70-71
Zen 70-71

acknowledgements

Cover: Neo Vision/Photonica; p. 8-9: Pinto/Zefa; p. 10-11: D. Chavkin/Stone; p. 13, 30, 59, 76-77, 94-95, 99, 104-105: Neo Vision/Photonica; p. 14-15: M. Thomsen/Zefa; p. 17, 18: © Akiko Ida; p. 20-21: M. Montezin/Marie Claire; p. 23: A. Tsunori/Option Photo; p. 27: E. Bernager/Marie Claire; p. 29: J. F. Jonvelle/Marie Claire; p. 33: M. Montezin/Marie Claire; p. 37: G. & M.D. de Lossy/Image Bank; p. 38-39: D. Robb/Stone; p. 40: P. Verdi/Option Photo; p. 42-43: B. Martin/Marie-Claire; p. 44-45: Fontshop D.R.; p. 48-49: J. Polillio/Stone; p. 51: E. Hauguel/Marie Claire; p. 57: G. Girardot/Marie Claire; p. 64 : A. Tsunori/Option Photo; p. 66-67: D.R.; p. 68-69: A. Parker/Option Photo; p. 81: G. Girardot/Marie Claire; p. 83: V. Besnault/Pix; p. 86-87: D. Chavkin/Stone; p. 89: A. Parker/Option Photo; p. 91: M. Montezin/Marie Claire; p. 96-97: J. Hicks/Pix; p. 101: B. Andersson/Marie Claire; p. 106: B. Andersson/Marie Claire; p. 109: E. Kohli/Marie Claire; p. 111: U. R. Lucky/Option Photo; p. 112: S. Lancrenon/Marie Claire; p. 116-117: Regine M./Image Bank; p. 118-119: Photonica; p. 121: H. Jullian/Marie Claire.

Illustrations: Marianne Maury Kaufmann pages 52, 54-55, 62-63, 70-71, 74-75.

60 tips

• ALL THE KEYS, ALL THE TIPS TO ANSWER ALL YOUR HEALTH QUESTIONS •

60 TIPS **allergies**

60 TIPS **anti-ageing**

60 TIPS **cellulite**

60 TIPS **detox**

60 TIPS **flat stomach**

60 TIPS **headaches**

60 TIPS **healthy skin**

60 TIPS **sleep**

60 TIPS **slimming**

60 TIPS **stress relief**

Editorial director: Caroline Rolland
Editorial assistant: Alexandra Bentz
Graphic design and layout: G & C MOI
Final checking: Fabienne Hélou
Illustrations: Alexandra Bentz
Production: Felicity O'Connor
Translation: JMS Books LLP

© Hachette Livre (Hachette Pratique) 2002
This edition published in 2004 by Hachette Illustrated UK, Octopus Publishing Group Ltd., 2–4 Heron Quays, London E14 4JP

English translation by JMS Books LLP (email: moseleystrachan@blueyonder.co.uk)
Translation © Octopus Publishing Group Ltd.

All rights reserved. No part of this publication may be reproduced in material form (including photocopying or storing it in any medium by electronic means and whether or not transiently or incidentally to some other use of this publication) without the written permission of the copyright owner, except in accordance with the provisions of the Copyright, Designs and Patents Act 1988 or under the terms of a licence issued by the Copyright Licensing Agency, 90 Tottenham Court Road, London W1P 9HE.

A CIP catalogue for this book is available from the British Library

ISBN: 1 84430 074 9

Printed in Singapore by Tien Wah Press